Praise for *A Time of Birds*

CW00554617

"Glorious ... an inspiring adv[...]
joyful times." Tom Chesshyr[...]

"A perfect read for these times of isolation ... a fantastic book."
John Toal, BBC Radio Ulster

"[A] wonderful narrative ... harrowing and inspiring by rapid turns
... Indispensable, heart-breaking, uplifting, beautifully conceived
and written." NI Arts Council

"A moving and thought-provoking set of meditations ... detailed,
vivid and lyrical" Patricia Carswell, *WI Magazine*

"Ideal reading for vicarious armchair travellers ... rich in emotional
flashbacks and keen observations ... Moat is an exquisite stylist.
Her unhurried, free-flowing narrative captivates the reader from the
very first sentence ... a thoroughly unputdownable travel book."
Vitali Vitaliev, *Engineering & Technology Magazine*

"A prayer of a book. A hymn to the healing power of cycling slow."
Chris Dolan

"A stand-out work of honesty and integrity, loss and hope, as
revealed through the seemingly simple act of turning the pedals on
a bicycle." Alan Brown

While the Earth Holds Its Breath

EMBRACING THE WINTER SEASON

Helen Moat

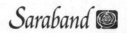

Published by Saraband,
3 Clairmont Gardens,
Glasgow, G3 7LW

www.saraband.net

ISBN: 9781916812321

Printed and bound in Great Britain by Clays Ltd, Elcograf S.p.A.

10 9 8 7 6 5 4 3 2

MIX
Paper | Supporting
responsible forestry
FSC® C018072

Contents

Contents

I dedicate this book to the people of Noto Peninsula, who welcomed me with such graciousness and kindness. On New Year's Day 2024, a year after I visited Ishikawa Prefecture, they suffered a devastating earthquake, followed by severe flooding the following September. Homes were once again destroyed and power and water cut off. The ruthlessness of nature in Japan tests the philosophy of wabi-sabi to the hilt — the acceptance of life's transience and imperfection.

My thoughts are with the people of Noto as they rebuild their lives.

Prologue:
In the Beginning

Kittilä

Every moment is a fresh beginning.
T.S. Eliot

I'm staring into the dark eye of the lake – tar black and freezing. I don't know the lake's name or where it lies on the map. I don't know if I've travelled north, south, east or west to reach it. I know I'd never find it again on my own. I also know I'm mesmerised by this place, and that I want to come back.

And in this moment, I feel the pull of the water's opaque underworld beneath the snow and ice. There's something bewitching about this small circle of water. The realisation startles me. Darkness is something negative. It absorbs all light, taking away the light that's essential for my well-being. It makes me dread the coming of winter every single year. Yet I've chosen to come to this place in the Arctic Circle where winter is at its darkest and coldest to sit on a ridiculously small camping stool at -20°C to fish for fish I'll never catch with a ridiculously small fishing rod. It doesn't matter, though. Here on my stool, surrounded by the polar night, I'm taken back to an existence before memory, a time when I floated gently in amniotic fluid, womb-dark and safe. Something primeval is happening to me as I cast and reel, some residue in my DNA of a time before memory when darkness was a constant in the other-world of womb. On this forest lake, the silence is all-encompassing, more acutely felt after the roar of our snowmobiles, the bright headlights and the sound of drilling as the Finns cut fishing holes for us with their ice augers. Now we're held in the silent rings of forest and lake, our camping stools arranged in a circle beside circular ice holes. Circles within circles.

I peer into the black water. Could there really be fish beneath the snow and ice? In this freezing water? My small plastic rod seems inadequate and so do my casting skills. But I don't mind: the night is cradling me. Across the lake, pine trees spill ink and snow. In this northern outpost of Finland, where city lights are far away and small settlements sparse, the sky is blue glass and stars crystal-cut. I feel adrift from myself and somehow anchored to the frozen land and arch of sky surrounding me, as if held in a snow dome. It's a strange sensation, but not an unpleasant one. The land may be silent, but it speaks to me: the raven eye of water, the ghost snow and butter moon.

Suddenly, I'm conscious of our hosts shuffling around us, checking lines, rubbing their hands together in their thick gloves or stamping their feet for warmth, but they don't utter a word: the Finns, I've been told, are known for their economic use of language. They'd brought us here on snow-mobiles from the small town of Levi through the polar night of the Lappish afternoon. We'd whooped and laughed as we leaned into bends or lost control of our machines. We'd been giddied by the power of our snowmobiles, by a sky flung with stars and frosted pine forests and moon-ghosted snow. The Finns had smiled wryly at our excitement. Now on the frozen lake, I concentrate on finding a bite. Every winter, I shrink from the darkness back home, but here on this lake, the land is holding me tenderly. Something is happening. In the stillness, the whitened trees and indigo-blue sky whisper to me. Flittering thoughts ease out; I have become one with the ghosted landscape. Now and again, there's the clickety-click of someone reeling in their line, or the squeak of snow underfoot as one of the guides moves around, checking our progress. But otherwise, time feels suspended. Frozen in the dark beauty of the Arctic Circle.

* * *

That winter at 67 degrees north, I learned Finnish Laplanders embrace the short days of winter. Even through the weeks of the polar night, *kaamos* – when the sun doesn't rise above the horizon and there's perpetual dusk and darkness – Finns spend as much time as possible outdoors. In Kittilä, we'd done the same. We – a group of travel journalists – had snow-shoed in a midday twilight of electric blue and plush pink. We'd climbed the hill above Levi late at night, small beneath a navy sky of constellations and the powdery sweep of the Milky Way. We'd waded through snow to the summit, giggling like teenagers and speaking in loud conspiratorial whispers before climbing onto a wooden fence to watch the horizon shimmer faintly with the grey-green of the aurora. We'd fallen silent, engrossed by the shapeshifting sky. It felt as though we'd sat on that fence for hours, just watching, although it was probably just a few minutes. We forgot each other, just as lost to the sky as we'd been to the lake. No one spoke. Once more, we'd been silenced by the Arctic night. That night, I lay in bed and watched the heavens rain stars over the glass roof of my cabin. Watching, watching. Being. Still lost to the sky.

Laplanders, I discovered on that trip, know the outdoors so intimately they sub-divide the seasons into eight: Frozen Winter, Crusted Snow, Melting Ice, Midnight Sun, Harvest, Autumn Foliage, First Snow and Polar Night. With the long months of darkness, the first snows falling as early as October and continuing until April, you'd think Laplanders would suffer from Seasonal Affective Disorder (SAD), but they told me it has little effect on them because the snow reflects light. The Finns I'd met in the Arctic Circle that year approached winter positively. They spent as much time outdoors in the polar night as on lighter days. They went out running, cycling, skiing and hiking in the dusk and darkness just as I'd seen on my trip.

Why were incidents of Seasonal Affective Disorder so strikingly low in the Arctic Circle? I asked myself back home. I needed to find out more and see what I could learn for myself. One researcher, Kari Leibowitz, had noted the residents of Tromsø – inside the Arctic Circle – maintain high rates of well-being, even between late November and late January when the sun never climbs above the horizon. She observed that northern Norwegians spend a lot of time in the outdoors – just as I'd seen with the Finns. The low rate of SAD in Lapland fits with the science that demonstrates being active and spending time outdoors boosts mood. Leibowitz also discovered an attitude of celebration in winter in Tromsø: winter was a season to be enjoyed, not endured! She reported a positive mindset towards the darkness. There were other factors at play too. Laplanders create warmth and cosiness indoors in the blackness of winter, just as squirrels insulate their dreys with leaves and twigs and moss. They also take comfort in friendships and in nature. It's what Norwegians call *kos*. I felt excited reading this research. It gave me hope. All of this I could do at home. I would mentally prepare myself for the winter season and approach it more mindfully. I could keep a journal and record my feelings about the darker months. I'd note what worked for me and what made me low. I'd keep a gratitude diary, focus on friendships, good food and creating an atmosphere of warmth inside my drafty Edwardian house.

Every year for as long as I could remember, I spiralled down into winter anxiety. Every autumn, I dreaded the shortening days, the grey skies, the fog and rain. But what if I went outdoors, even on the worst days, instead of turning my back on winter weather? I would try to embrace the Finnish way of winter. Would it work without the light-giving snow? Could I learn to love the drizzle and mists? I didn't know, but I would reinvent winter in my mind. If I could. I'd had enough of being prisoner to grey skies and low moods. *Every moment is a fresh moment*, T.S. Eliot had written. I would make a new journey into winter, a mindful journey, a hopeful journey, one of celebration. This was my fresh moment, and as I made the decision, I felt something lighten inside me.

The First Winter

A Winter of Small Things

October

The Sea, the Sea

There is a rapture on the lonely shore.
– Lord Byron

It was the beginning of October. I was on edge. It was a familiar feeling. Summer days filled with light already seemed far away, even though just a few weeks ago I'd basked in hot sunshine. Below us, the coastal uplands of Carmarthenshire fell away to the Taf Estuary and the Dylan Thomas town of Laugharne. Outside, the Welsh rain fell soft and persistent, water streaming down the windows of our campervan. I sighed and wrapped myself in the duvet, wiping the window so that I could follow the lines of hedgerows and trees to the *Under Milk Wood* town. Far below, the remains of its medieval castle and tumble of dark stone, whitewashed and pastel-painted cottages lay hidden from sight. Beyond, Dylan's writing shed lay on the shore. Thomas had been inspired by the Taf. I hoped it would inspire me too, even in the light-mean mizzle. The writer had written pulsing prose here, and desperate begging letters to clear his debts. Nights, he'd pickled his liver in one of the town's three pubs, ear-wigging on conversations, scribbling furiously on notepaper or napkins, catching the gossip, catching the peculiarities of the town's characters, capturing the absurdities and beauty of life. I was determined I would embrace the beauty of the estuary too, even in the cold rain.

In the morning, the mist lay low in Laugharne. We set out with my sister and her family for Dylan's writing shed along the estuary shoreline. The damp sea mist wrapped us in a soggy blanket. How different from the previous Easter when my husband Tom and I had come here, the sun gentle and full of promise for a long summer ahead. The long ascending call of the curlew had gurgled from the mudflats, the orange beaks and legs of oystercatchers splashing colour on the salt-marshes. Surrounding Carmarthen Bay are shallow inlets and bays, exposing mudflats and sandflats at low tide. The estuary marshes are filled with the small life of sea vegetation and animals. Salicornia thrives in the mudflats – also known as glasswort, pickleweed, picklegrass, marsh samphire, sea beans and sea asparagus. Cockles, blue mussel beds, purple sea grass and sea lavender, waders and river lamprey give life to these waters. The rhythms of the estuary also gave life to Thomas's writing. Back on that spring day, we'd peered into the locked boat shed with its writing desk and visited the boathouse, white laundry flapping in the breeze as if Dylan and Caitlin Thomas were still at home.

Now on the cusp of winter, we battled the moisture-laden wind on the shoreline. *Here we go again*, I thought. It was difficult not to compare the estuary to that spring when the earth was stirring, and the air was gently warming. I felt the weight of the darkening skies as I bowed my head against the weather, the dampness clawing my hair, drizzle on my lashes. *I hate it, I hate it, I hate it.* But then I remembered my pledge to change my mindset towards winter. I stopped to gaze out at the bay. As the clouds stretched and thinned, the creep of light spread across the bay, darkening again as the clouds closed in. There was no Arctic Circle light-giving snow, but the sea was reflecting light. I watched the interplay between light and dark with the scudding of the clouds. The estuary was animated, brightening and dulling under the flow of sky, flowing and ebbing with the tide. *No, don't hate it*, I thought to myself. *Embrace it.* In that moment, I gave myself up to the energy of the tides, the currents in the estuary, the cold rain drizzling down my cheeks, the edge-of-winter coastal air sharp on my face. There was *rapture* on this shore, a feeling of joy, a coming to, an awakening I experienced every time I looked out at the sea. I breathed deep, taking in mouthfuls of salty air. I was alive! The Arctic Circle was too far away to visit, but ocean lay all around me on my island. It wouldn't be difficult to travel to the coast over winter, to re-energise in the light and the thrust of the sea. I was already scribbling a new narrative of winter inside my head – one to note in my winter journal.

The boathouse and museum were closed so we pushed back through the rain to our campervan and brewed tea. We were aware we were too close, all too aware of Covid-19. When the others left, Tom and I thought of returning to the field on the hilltop for one more night, but the rain was coming down heavier, relentless in its downpour. We beat it up the motorway back to Derbyshire, spray reducing our vision to white water. But if we'd known that the coast was going to be out of bounds most of that winter, I think we would have lingered. We'd have embraced the rain and the underlining of another summer. I'd have stored up the energy of the Welsh waters. That short weekend by the sea was an early winter gift that would soon be taken from me. I just didn't know it yet. I didn't know either that imposed solitude would bring other gifts, or that, when the world opened again, I would travel across the planet from The Arctic Circle again to the Land of the Rising Sun to find out how to love the dark.

Shinrin Yoku –
The Japanese Art of Forest Bathing

The clearest way into the universe is through a forest wilderness.
– John Muir

Once I had a Japanese pen pal from the northern tip of Honshu. Takako sent me gifts: gossamer tissue paper, bitter green tea and wooden dolls dressed in the seasons – spring blossom, summer daisies, autumn leaves and snowflakes. And letters, written on thin air-mail paper, describing a life impossibly exotic. The culture of Japan drew me to it, its elegance, rituals and natural beauty, although I'd never been. I lost touch with Takako, but Japan continued to send me its gifts: sushi tasting of the sea, fantastical Ghibli animations, zany manga comics, delicate origami and gardens of poetry.

And *shinrin yoku* – the art of forest bathing.

October was sliding inescapably towards November, slipping out of my grasp, and I still felt a resistance to the approach of winter from somewhere deep in the core of my body. *Slow down*, I wanted to shout. *I'm not ready for you.* But November I knew would elbow in. The Welsh coast had invigorated me, even in the rain. And now my dreams were filled with the Taf. Was the estuary not at its most alive in winter with overwintering waders and waterfowl flocking to its shores? If only it didn't take several hours to reach it from my home. If only I didn't live right in the centre of my island, almost as far away from the sea as you could get.

Forest bathing offered an alternative to the sea. Woodlands and forest plantations were all around me, several within walking distance. I couldn't bathe in sunlight most days, but forest bathing I could do even on the gloomiest winter days. I just wasn't sure what it was.

I set out to find out more, discovering the Japanese sought out trees to restore their sense of well-being and to find peace and equilibrium. Some travel to Nijino Matsubara on Karatsu Bay, a 360-year-old forest, known as the *Black Pine Forest of One Million Trees;* others to the Bamboo Forest near Kyoto and Aokigahara at the foot of Mount Fuji, the *Sea of Trees* with its porous lava floor eerily absorbing sound. Or they may simply walk from their office to a tree-filled city park at lunchtime. The idea of forest bathing neither involves dipping in a forest stream nor sunbathing in a woodland clearing, I discovered. It's simply immersing yourself in forest, soaking in its atmosphere. By the early 1990s, forest bathing had become part of the Japanese government's national health programme. Trees, Japanese scientists had observed, boosted mood, energy levels and the immune system; reduced anxiety, improved sleep and lowered blood pressure. With winter anxiety and the existential threat of Covid, Japanese forest bathing would surely be an antidote to my winter unease. I could not afford to go to Japan, but I could do some Japanese forest bathing in the heart of England.

The Churnet Valley lies on the edge of the Peak District, not far from the pottery town of Stoke-on-Trent. It's a place of densely wooded valleys and high meadows. When we arrived, there was a winter chill in the air. We set out into the woods, passing a pond of ornamental ducks and a black swan, autumn trees splashing gold on the surface of the water. The path widened out and we continued upwards through beech trees beside Wom Brook. The flow of water over stone was a lullaby, the autumn trees a bright wall hanging. It wasn't the *Black Pine Forest of One Million Trees* or the bamboo *Sea of Trees*. It was a decidedly English forest: small, compact and intimate.

There was something primitive about walking these woods. As we dropped back down into Ousal Dale, I stopped. I breathed. I turned my head upwards. The larches soaring over my head were youngsters in comparison to the ancient forests of Japan. But still they felt primal, trunks breaking the sky, closing in around me in wigwam formation, light bursting through fiery orange tops. I circled round, cradled by the conifers, the core strength of their trunks so rooted to the earth, rooting me. That residual recognition of the womb again. What was it about the geometry of their lines and the shafts of light falling to the forest floor that stirred my soul so?

I breathed out. My heartbeat slowed. My breath came even. My nose filled with the scent of pine and sticky sap. My ears tuned into the sigh of leaves and the faint *pip-pip-pip* of a long-tailed tit. I felt the tension leave my body. I was bathing in forest. Woodland was healing, John Muir, the father of National Parks, observed – long before the Japanese government had prescribed forest bathing. I would make them my home on the most anxious of winter days.

The Earth Holds its Breath

How many lessons of faith and beauty we should lose,
if there were no winter in our year?
– Thomas Wentworth Higginson

In winter, plant life withers away, skies empty of birds, animals go underground. Forests are silent. That was my perception, anyway. I always thought of death when I looked at the skeletal outlines of trees, fingers of bone reaching for pewter skies, their leaves cast away, mottled and crisped on the ground, or soggy from rain. I watched bright autumn golds, reds and purples drain of colour over winter, wizen and disintegrate, leaving laces of veins. Was there another way of reading nature? Of course there was. But I had yet to go on that journey.

Away from the sea and the woods, I felt my energy drain away. I sensed the looming edge of winter, and I too was on edge. I had to remind myself every day I was in charge of the winter narrative inside my head, and on the pages of my journal. Sometimes I felt in control of the story, sometimes not. As autumn colour threatened to give way to the muted palate of winter, the old lethargy returned. Outside, there were moments of pure joy, days of bright sunshine and long, deep shadows emphasising the soft contours of the land. On days like these, the cold air needled my throat and face, making me feel the blood surge through my body. But there were more days when the Earth was so still, it felt like it was holding its breath. When the rain clouds and mists hung low, I felt suffocated.

I tried to remember when I started to feel repelled by winter. Had it begun in childhood? I had no memory of disliking it. Memories of the months that bookended Christmas in Ireland were warm ones: occasional days of snow, sledging on scrap metal, post-war Christmas décor and gifts, hot stews and roast beef with mustard on a Friday night, warm soda bread. I loved toasting bread on our open fire. I remember discovering a hibernating hedgehog beneath builders' bricks. I don't remember going out much – darkness fell around four on the shortest days and we stayed indoors. I was fascinated by my breath on the air of my unheated bedroom on days when the temperature dipped below zero, the windows icing up on the inside, heavy piles of blankets like a ton weight on my body and a stinging hot water bottle. Rain, I remembered. It was always raining on my Irish island, and I hated it even back then. But most memories were of spring and summer. Did we ever visit the sea in winter, or take long walks? I don't remember doing so. I remember seasonal activities – picking primroses, scoping frogspawn into jam jars, summer sea swims, chestnut, blackberry, mushroom and rosehip picking – but I don't remember an awareness of the circular nature of life, the constant turning of the seasons. Each season slid so slowly into the next, it felt as if a single year lasted a decade back then. I was too young to appreciate the constant turning, turning, turning. So when did it start, this feeling of impending gloom that kicked in at the beginning of autumn? Sometime in adulthood, I guessed. It must have been a gradual thing that worsened with each passing year, barely noticeable to begin with. *Did anyone love winter anyway?* I wondered. I asked fellow writers in a group chat how they felt about it. Some favoured it, to my surprise, over all the seasons. They talked about time spent in the European Alps, Siberia, Russia and Ukraine. In the northern hemisphere, there were countries with proper frozen winters, I acknowledged, but then there were the mild winters of the British Isles warmed by the Gulf Stream. These days, we only experienced a handful of snowy days when the snow melted as quickly as it arrived, and clear frosted skies were a rarity on our grey-capped island.

'I love the cosiness and being wrapped up in blankets with a good book or film; the food, which is so hearty and warming; and I love a rainy day,' someone pointed out. There was agreement.

'The rain on a walk means fewer people. The solitary feeling on a cold wet day is a great pleasure in winter.' I too had started to walk alone on cold, dreary days when there were fewer people out and found I could tune into nature without distraction, but I still avoided the rain. I promised myself I would try it.

But one answer stopped me in my tracks: 'It's my favourite season – for reflection among other things.'

'I like the idea of winter reflection,' I replied.

'Yes, only the winter's dark nights and cold weather slow us down...a gift from nature?'

A gift from nature.

The idea of following an inner winter journey had been planted inside my head. I remembered how a Finn had talked about mental preparation for winter – a change in gear so that he could slow down and take time to rest. But still I clung to the idea of healing in the outdoors. And like most of the other winter lovers I'd communicated with, I sought out those brighter days and waited for the snow.

The Buzzards

If you truly love nature, you will find beauty everywhere.
– Vincent van Gogh

There was a single cry in the air. I looked up to see two buzzards circling the sky high above our town. They glided on an updraft of air, the feathered ends of tails and wings splayed in avian magnificence. The heft of wing seemed at odds with the easy grace of their movements. One dropped like a plumb line to its quarry on the valley floor below.

My mood had been low that morning. The old negative feelings towards winters were winning the battle and I was feeling helpless in my despondency. This was going to be a difficult struggle to overcome. And now, walking alone up Salters Lane, a tunnel of green with a glint of autumn gold, anxiety was trailing me. Would my sons, PhD students, be able to come home for Christmas? How long would this second wave of Covid last? Would we be locked down again? How would I get through the long winter ahead?

But the buzzards pulled me into the present. I stood motionless, caught in the flight of these birds of prey – their constant circling, focused searching and patient waiting. Gliding, diving. Gliding, circling. And in that moment, the buzzards and I were in harmony, both absorbed in the here and now.

Me watching the buzzards; the buzzards watching their prey.

I climbed on up the hill to reach a rough track that led onto the crest of Masson Hill. I paused at the spot where Patrick, my son, and I had drunk coffee from a flask early in the spring, when the country had first gone into lockdown.

We'd gazed out at the town spread out at our feet, then to the Peak beyond. We could see Darley Dale and the junction of the valley, heading off to Chatsworth in one direction and to Bakewell in the other. And beyond that, the Dark Peak with its edges and moorlands, fading out to a blue smudge on the horizon. And with a buzzard's eye, our world had expanded beyond the limits of our lockdown. That day, I'd thought, *This is enough! This is more than enough.*

Back in the present, I continued along the track, the animated voices of four climbers – or maybe cavers – behind me, hard hats and rucksacks autumn orange-bright. They headed down towards the quarry while I cut across the meadow to a thicket enclosed by a circular wall. Patrick and I had explored it that spring day, marvelling at the mysterious spiral of daffodils and the circle of stones among the beeches. We guessed it was a spot New Age Pagans used. Now on the cusp of winter, the gnarled branches of beeches were covered in moss and lichen, their trunks darkened to mud green. There was a sense of abandonment in this copse. It wasn't beautiful but it had something that calmed my mind. The enclosure was womb-like with its rounded outer stone wall and shadowy darkness. Venturing deeper into the grove, I found the floor of the woodland was covered in craters – three to six feet deep in places. Gingerly, I walked the rims of the holes, not wanting to fall in. I fell into the enclosure's stillness. I felt its history. This place had surely been mined for lead. Who knew what lay at the base of the holes under the ground ivy? – possibly mine-shafts, dropping hundreds of feet into the belly of the hill. Masson was covered in them. Old documents recorded curious names: Ringing Rake; Toadstool Bank; Jiggling Box; Old Jant Mine; Queen Shaft and Gentlewoman's Pipe.

I left the copse and tumbled off the hillside, down to Salters Lane again. Walking alone was something I'd never readily done; I preferred the companionship of others, the shared experience. But in walking alone, I realised my only communion was with nature – with the buzzards and jackdaws, their harsh cries filling the air, and the robins threading the hedges with their subdued winter song. I remembered the frozen fishing lake at Kittilä, and how I'd felt at one with the snowy forest and star-filled sky. This was a meditation I could practise at home. I just needed to tune into the dales and moorlands, the skies of resident birds, the meadows and hedgerows, and forests.

As I reached the bottom of the hill, a burst of sunshine filled the valley. A burst of serotonin. A burst of endorphins. My mood soared with the buzzards above my head.

End of Season Fruits

*Don't judge each day by the harvest you reap
but by the seeds you plant.*
– Robert Louis Stevenson

Throughout October, I continued to pick the cherry tomatoes in my garden, little jewels of red now hanging onto life. How I nurtured those little fruits, as if in nurturing them I could hold onto summer. They had started to mature late in the session towards the end of September, too late to catch the heat of summer. I put the riper ones on my kitchen windowsill and wrapped the paler orange and yellow fruit tenderly in newspapers, placing them in a paper bag with an apple in the airing cupboard. At first progress was slow, then towards the middle of October, after I'd switched on the heating, I checked in on my patients. Gently, I unfolded each blanket of newspaper to find each one a juicy red. A miracle! Even the dark green ones had turned fully red. It felt like Christmas: each tomato a gift of colour, each tomato a physical memory of summer.

That evening, I made cherry tomato tartlets, placing the tomatoes in a nest of shortcrust pastry with fried onions and goat's cheese. Each mouthful of cherry was a burst of sunshine, juicy and full of flavour.

Towards the end of October, I made the last tomato, onion and goat's cheese tartlets and flavoursome tomato salads with mozzarella and fresh basil. I picked the remaining green tomatoes before the frosts set in and made chutney. All the ingredients were thrown into the pot: red onion, garlic, ginger, cardamom seeds and brown sugar. The windows steamed up and the smell of sweet and sour and spice filled the room. The mixture simmered to a treacle-coloured gloop. I spooned it into jam jars as saffron-coloured leaves floated past the French doors from the cherry tree.

On our Peak District walks, the cheese and ham spread with homemade chutney in nutty bread tasted even better after a climb – my tomato chutney accompanied with woodland, gritstone edge and moorland. Summer fed our early winter rambles.

* * *

My neighbour left a bag of apples on my doorstep. My own tiny apple tree, ridiculously weighed down with outsized apples the previous winter – filling my freezer with stacked containers of cooked apples to keep us going in steaming puddings through a long, rain-filled winter – had not produced one single apple this year. I was grateful for Colin's offering.

I took his apples inside and returned to the garden, where I'd been raking up leaves, ignoring the wintry weather. I put on my headphones and listened to Vivaldi's *Four Seasons: Winter* as I worked. This was no subdued piece. The violin didn't come in *largo* – slow and stately – or *piano*, quietly and gently. It came in fast and furious, the notes a tumble of energy, depicting gusts of wind or the dance of a snow-storm. I worked vigorously, roused by the energy of the music. There was a great deal of winter joy in Vivaldi's first movement. Surely Vivaldi was a winter lover along with all the other seasons? The cold rain, stinging my face, the wind and music were shaking me out of my Sunday morning lethargy. How good the fresh air felt. How much better the warmth felt when I went finally went back indoors. In the kitchen, I set about making a crumble with my neighbour's apples. I prepared the sweet the Scandinavian way: crisp apples – not too cooked – smothered in cinnamon, sugar, walnuts and sultanas. I covered the crumble with slivers of butter and dusted them with brown cane sugar to make the topping crunchy. I closed the curtains against the dark and cold, the summer of fruit brought inside. I lifted my spoon and tasted a burst of apple, sticky sultana, crunchy nut and spice. The steaming crumble with cream was *hygge* in a bowl. No self-respecting Scandinavian or northern European would ever think of dieting in winter. Food is comfort against cold and dark.

Rambles in the Dark

The power of imagination makes us infinite.
– John Muir

It was Emma who started the rambles in the dark. Those night-time walks were born on a sunlit afternoon's ramble, just before the longer evenings of summer ebbed away. On that end-of-summer walk, we'd followed the clip-clop of horse along Hackney Lane before switch-backing up a narrow, traffic-free road. Ameycroft Lane had a dreamy, bygone feel to it, enclosed by high mossy walls and earthen banks knitted with roots. That day, red berries shining brightly in the sunshine, I tried not to think about the fact that summer was slipping away.

'We could walk every week right through autumn and winter,' Emma suggested.

As we headed down towards All Saints Church, I thought about that previous winter of rain, when I'd barely left the house. I'd curled up dormouse-like under the duvet; sluggish, sleepy, drifting in shadows, aching for light. This winter could be different.

'Let's do it,' I said.

Days are where we must live, even in winter, but it didn't have to be a prison of house and walls. I needed the rush of air, the slap of wind on my cheeks. I needed to feel alive. Outdoors. It was just difficult to motivate myself in the dark months, when the black descended so early.

A mutual friend, Sue, joined us for what Emma called our 'ladies' walks'. At the end of our tramp, we stopped by the chestnut tree, conkers spilling the ground, a scattering of orange leaf.

'I know what's going to happen,' Emma said. 'Ian will want to come.'

'He could come in disguise, slip into one of your dresses. No one will notice. Never mind the beard.'

Quietly, Emma dropped the 'ladies' from the Ladies' Walking Group in our group chat and invited our men. From then on, five of us walked through the daylight into the gloaming and on into the darkness of October evenings.

* * *

On our first men-allowed autumn-into-winter walk, Sue led, marching us along the jitties of the Bank into Lumsdale on the other side of town, black leaking through the sky, colour draining from the landscape. We forded stepping stones across the brook, the water pale in the gloaming. In the dusk, sounds intensified, the trickle of water like glass. Leaves crackled underfoot; our voices sharp on the night air. Above us, the forest turned to ink. We did a circle of eight and dropped down to the falls, high metal fences gleaming in the twilight, keeping Coronavirus out. We tramped the lane that ran parallel to the gorge with its narrow pathway, ruined mills, leats, flues and wheel pit, and climbed the cobbled path up the hill again. The light faded out. I switched on my head torch, its beam catching the worn stone of the path. This was the beginning of a new relationship with the dark: the sense of smell and sound were *large* in the dark, as sight was hindered. It was exhilarating.

With vision reduced, my imagination grew. That noise in the undergrowth? Was it a badger or a fox? The rustle by the stream? A water vole? The whisper in the trees? Woodland nymphs! I remembered again what it was to have the imagination of a child. I'd always been a dreamer, living inside my head and creating my own worlds. I infuriated adults, especially my teachers. Now tapping into my imagination in the dark, I was that child again.

When it poured all afternoon a week later, we did not duck out of our Tuesday night walk. Crossing the town park, we followed the Derwent. The river was full, and the sound of rushing water filled the twilight after a day of rain. The light of the Victorian lamps fell on the pathway, now sodden with damp autumn leaves. There was just enough light in the gloaming to make out red iron oozing through paler limestone in the cliff face.

'It tells us there were once deserts and gullies here,' Tom, my geologist husband, informed me, and I marvelled at the idea that my soggy Matlock was once a dry and arid place.

Up on Pic Tor, we paused to view the town's houses stretched out across the Bank with their little squares of yellow light surrounding County Hall and its metal crown. Our town looked ethereal in the half-light, yet warm and inviting. Careering down the other side of the hillside into the graveyard, we tried not to skid on the grassy path that led to sagging graves – no ghostly figures in the gloaming – and slipped safely out the lychgate.

Back on the Bank, we climbed the ancient meadows of Denefields, an island of green in among the town houses, then plunged into the darkness of oak, hazel and birch. The night had caught us in this tunnel of darkness. It was beautifully eerie, and quiet but for the hum of traffic and the *mek- mek-mek* of a blackbird. Why had we never thought of walking our town on the cusp of darkness before, when the streets and jitties were empty, and the twilight belonged only to us?

Back home, I felt revitalised. There was no need to fear the darkness, no need to fear the onslaught of winter. I would embrace it. Step outside.

With each subsequent week, the darkness fell earlier, autumn colour deepened, leaves drifted, paths became gold. It was Ian's turn to lead. The steep jitty leading up the side of the old Jackson House Hydro was already gloomy with the gathering dusk. Soon, we were climbing into woodlands, peering into ink. We followed the boundary of Hurker Wood along a drystone wall and turned east along a track leading through Scots, Corsican and lodgepole pines.

We fell into silence for a while, focusing on negotiating a stretch of boggy ground. Mud gave way to sandy earth covered in pine needles. The ground felt easy underfoot; soft, with a little give. But then the level track fell steeply off the hillside. I grabbed tree trunks as gravity pulled me off the hang. The remaining light ebbed away as we descended the forest. We switched our head torches on, beams illuminating the barks of textured trunks. The night wrapped a blanket around the pines; around us. Shapes became blurry. The blackened land merged with the sky. Black on black. Our world was now a place of fantasy. I was growing to love the dark.

* * *

Night devoured day. The clocks went back. By late afternoon, darkness was descending. Winter was marching in. The winds blustered in bursts, stripped leaves, exposed branches. The remaining leaves drooped, soggy and lifeless. There would be no more walks through the gloaming into the night; no more watching the light ease out. We would step out into the black.

After a day of rain, the skies cleared. We had a new sky-scape for our walks: a three-quarter moon made of silk. A desert orange planet by its side. A sky stitched with starry sequins.

Tom was leading. He had pondered a route over a narrow railway bridge, a slippery plank of narrow wood between the track and the river below. An imagined slip in the dark-ness and freezing water below was a warning; we turned right, away from the bridge and along the White Peak Loop towards Rowsley. A circle of light appeared in the night, a cyclist, then four more circles. Runners. After that, there was just us and the trail. Our world was reduced to footfall – footfall and stars. We left the trail and climbed a slip of a path between beech hedges. Our torch lights shrank the world to small detail: a heap of leaves; a trough of water; a slice of thicket.

'This is the brightest Mars has been in around twenty years,' Ian said. Astronomy was a passion he shared with Tom. Both geologists, they loved their rocks, big and small, on Earth and in the sky. Tom as a child had met astronomer Patrick Moore – had been starstruck as Moore signed a copy of a space book. He invited Tom to write to him, to tell him about his discoveries.

And what a journey this child had gone on. How lucky he had been to discover space at the end of the sixties. Seven-year-old Tom had watched Apollo 11 take off with elation. This would be the one. Man *would* land on the moon. History *would* be made. Apollo 10 in May of that year had nearly crashed into the moon. A fire in the cabin of Apollo

1, two years earlier, had killed three astronauts. It was a space soap, a drama unfolding. But this time, it *was* different. *This time*, man landed, human feet contacted the moon. History was made. Tom watched the television footage of Apollo 11 touching down. He listened to those thrilling words *The Eagle has landed*, watched Armstrong step onto the surface of the moon – a man *really* on the moon and no cheese in sight. He heard the garbled words, later transcribed —not spontaneous but considered like poetry – *That's one small step for man, and one giant leap for mankind.* And one small boy felt privilege in the presence of living history.

But it was the year before that had captured Tom's imagination, sent him off on his own quest to discover space. On Christmas Eve of 1968, six-year-old Tom stood in the small world of his tenement flat somewhere in the East End of Glasgow. In his sixties' kitchen, he heard the news: Apollo 8 was circling the dark side of the moon. In that moment, Tom looked out the window, saw the moon in the sky high above Glasgow, and marvelled that Apollo 8 was out there in real time, brushing the moon. *Here, now!* And his world grew exponentially. It was the best Christmas present he could imagine.

I looked at Mars in the here and now. It appeared to outshine every other star in the sky. Even Jupiter was eclipsed by its orange glow.

'Why is Mars so bright just now?' I asked Tom.

'It's because we're lined up directly between it and the sun this month, so we're as close as we get to Mars.'

We followed the silk-moon off-cut and the sparkle of Mars across the valley and home. Yes, I was learning to love the dark. In obscuring our world, it revealed others.

* * *

We thought we'd walk on through winter into spring and on into summer across four seasons. But our walks would end abruptly. Covid was the reason we'd started the walks; Covid was the reason they would end. Those Tuesday evenings had given us something virtual meetings couldn't provide: the joy of human contact in the real world. Then a second lockdown was announced. We were told we could only walk with one other person outside our household. Emma suggested a final walk twice as long. Tom and I made cake and heated a bottle of Swedish mulled fruit juice for our final get-together. The label told me *Vintersaga is a serene shelter from the winter cold. Enjoy a Swedish winter moment.* Temperatures had dropped. Fierce winds had tried to whip our poly greenhouse away the previous day. Stubborn leaves, clinging to our cherry tree, were torn off.

'Take warm coats,' one of the messages said. 'I've been out all afternoon and it's Baltic.'

'Chilly,' said Sue.

Emma warned us it would be muddy, and rain was forecast.

'We'll wrap up warm,' I said. 'Time for winter skiing or mountaineering clothing.'

'Might leave our route with Mountain Rescue,' Emma joked.

But the rain stopped, and the wind died away. And we stepped out into our island mild rather than harsh Scandinavian cold. We walked through two woodlands, splashed through hillside run-off, squelched through mud. On the height, a fat moon threaded through the pines, stalking us across the plantation.

'A gibbous moon,' Ian said, who, like Tom, collected words along with rocks, books and records.

The moon was on the wane now, a sliver of silk snipped away. Mars was still prominent, appearing higher in the sky. Scots pines leaned into us as if to protect us in serene shelter. If it hadn't been for Covid, would we have lasted this long? The physical presence of friends had become important.

Now, I was experiencing night as my Stone Age ancestors had done: the chill of winter's approach, shadowy nature in the moonlight – the ever-present night at the entrance of their cave. The stars would have been even brighter then. There were no torches to guide their way in the dark, as we had, just the sky's lights. They were much closer to nature than modern man, much closer to the rhythms of the day and night. They lived in a world that didn't know man-made sounds. There were no cars, no planes, no sounds of machinery. Covid had given me a taster of that. Sweet, sweet stillness, a new awareness of nature's detail and the subtle changes in the turning of the seasons. Beauty on the edge of winter. The chill in the dark made me feel more alive; the stars, the moon, the charcoal of trees. As we stumbled through the woodland, I felt the intimacy of the night sky, bright, bright away from the glare of streetlights. I felt the intimacy of the trees, the hug of the pines. I felt the intimacy of detail picked out by my headtorch: a snaking root, a mossy branch, the glint of a rounded gritstone. I felt the intimacy of our friendship – five friends sharing cake, a spicy drink, the woodland, the moon, the stars and the sky. As we dropped down off the hillside, I felt the thrill of the black, the sense of danger from not being able to see what was all around me. Joy surged through my whole being; I was alive, alive,

alive. Winter's long hours of darkness, forcing us out into the evening after work, had given us this gift.

Three mountain bikers cycled by, breaking our mood, almost blinding us with their lights and kicking up mud. Their calls bounced round the woodland as they shouted warnings to each other of obstacles.

'Is mountain biking in the dark a thing?' I asked in wonder.

They disappeared into the night and the stillness of the woodland flowed over us again. We walked in easy silence, the only sound the crunch of last year's dried-out leaves underfoot. The pencil lines of tree trunks shone pale in our torch lights, everything beyond dark and unknowable.

Then, a crashing in the undergrowth.

'A badger!' Emma said. 'A young one!'

On the town's edge, we said our last goodbyes, hoping the lockdown would only last a month as promised. But while the human world was uncertain, the world of forest, hill and animal was immutable. The Earth orbiting the Sun, the moon orbiting the Earth. Nocturnal animals emerging in the winter dark to snuffle in the undergrowth.

Boundaries

Contentment comes from many great and small acceptances in life.
— Anonymous

Under Covid restrictions, Tom and I walked the boundaries of the Peak District National Park. The ten-mile stretch from Millford to Beeley offered up a distilled Peak of woods, moorland and water. A healing. Beech, birch and oak grounded me, water sang to me, and blustery moorland and edges blew my winter melancholy away. It was a walk in happiness. We wriggled in and out of the boundaries of the park. Its border guiding us, but not always containing us. Covid had given us restrictions, but my heart was being blown wide open. I felt vulnerable but the vulnerability rejuvenated me. The world seemed bigger, brighter and more intense in the low light, the edges of hills sharpened, waters clearer, the clouds edged with luminosity. I noted it in my gratitude diary. I was mentally preparing myself for winter's imminent arrival.

As we set out, the path was flooded with light and the leaves of beeches sang their colours – a farewell gift of dazzling leaf, a winter sweetener. Heading into Bank Wood, I tuned into the music of the woodland – the song of the burbling brook and meadow pipit song cascading through the valley. The brook forked and we forded a stream to climb through Smeekley Wood, then climbed Hewetts Bank onto uplands. Black jewels of blackberries still thrived on the heights. We plucked and ate a handful, screwing up our mouths at their bitterness, perversely enjoying their sweet-sour taste.

We scrambled onto Birchen Edge, ascending breathlessly through rock towers until we were on top of the escarpment. Beyond, the moorlands rippled out to higher points like waves on a shore. Birches twisted their silvered trunks skyward, the crowns of larch mustard yellow. We were in a landlocked Derbyshire of watery references. Three large rocks, their ends like the pointed brows of ships, were carved with the words 'Victory', 'Defiance' and 'Soverin'. Further along the edge, we came to a needle-thin monument, a memorial to Admiral Nelson and his sea-faring battles.

On the broad moorland track of Gibbet Moor, the world expanded to blocks of moorland and forest, then shrank in its detail. Sunshine warmed the backs of ginger Aberdeen Angus. Stonechats rose out of the heather and a gang of stoats came running hell for leather towards us on the forest track before braking to a halt and diving for cover. For a moment, I thought I was in a cartoon. The stoats set me off on a fit of giggles. I felt as giddy as a kid. Further on, hen harriers circled a plantation of conifers. I watched them glide on the air and marvelled at the effortlessness of their flight. At Hob Hurst's House – not a hobbit house but a Bronze Age burial mound – a buzzard soared on muscular wings, eyes like lasers. I wrote in my gratitude diary: *I've found the small child in me again. I'm seeing the world with fresh eyes.*

At Beeley Plantation, we descended a silvered world of forest and waterfall. Sunlight streamed through larch and pines, the moss of rock curtaining the ravine. Birdsong was quiet. The forest quiet but the rustle of departing leaves, the glassy fall of water far below. We met the lane dropping down to Beeley. A family were sitting in their smallholding, cradling cups of hot drinks on the makeshift terrace of their hut, wood smoke rising from the chimney, children chasing each other around a woodpile and stone oven, sunlight back-lighting the small woodland behind the pasture. It felt as if we'd walked into rural Romania, but instead we dropped into a quintessential English estate village.

I thought about the family on their smallholding as we walked through the cottages of Beeley, a scene of bucolic serenity. When I was growing up, my father told me the greatest thing was contentment. The walks I'd taken with him were not a march but an amble. Between the footsteps that grounded us to the earth, the rhythm and the forward thrust of movement, there was space to breathe, to pause, to watch, to listen and touch. I didn't understand it then. Contentment felt like containment to me. Joy, yes. Excitement, yes. But contentment? I wanted to expand my world, explore far-flung places, have adventure. But here was my father telling me I should be content with what I had.

I need to stop walking and pause; I thought in Beeley. *I need to still my heart, linger in autumn-into-winter's detail and in the sweep of nature's greatness.* Water, edge, woodland and moor: they provided it all.

* * *

When we returned to Beeley to walk to Winster, still on the boundary of the Peak District, the ground was recoloured with autumn russets, mustards, burnt orange, maroons and beige. In Rowsley Wood, we found a world of footbridges and tumbling streams, quarry faces and spoil tips – stone used for the stately home of Chatsworth House. Across the valley, Hillcarr Wood was an impressionist painting of dabbled colour and running paint – copper and ironised greens that blended with the beech trees in front of them. Old millstones lay abandoned on the pathway, thick with moss. The stones of ruined buildings had surrendered to lichen and fern. This was a dark, dank and mysterious place. A bypasser asked me – to my alarm – if I'd like to be murdered. He told me about a story of a killing on this spot. I'd entered a dark fable. The oddness of the encounter unnerved me. It also fed my imagination for story writing. As we walked on, the woodland floor lay thick with beech leaves. Tom and I rested on the foundation walls of a ruin. I tuned into the veins of leaves, the mottled hues of rock faces, the smooth green trunks of beeches, the silver lines of birch trunks and the long shadows in the dips of meadows. October had revealed a world of pattern and beauty. It had eased me through the transition of summer into winter. It had given me colour, the drift of leaf and soft autumn mists. It was carrying me gently into harder, darker, more melancholic days. One day, one step at a time, I would make my journey on into winter, knowing the cyclical nature of the seasons brought light and shade, rest and reflection: a journey into the inward self, then, rejuvenation in spring – an awakening – and with it all an equilibrium.

November

Bonds

He that is thy friend indeed; he will help thee in thy need.
– William Shakespeare

When does winter properly begin? For some, it's the beginning of December – meteorological winter, for others at Winter Solstice. For many, it feels winter has already begun when the clocks go back, and evenings are robbed of light. For me, it's when with the first hard frost arrives.

Frost comes hand in hand with clear starlit nights. On the fourth of November, I woke to bright skies, silvered earth and the remaining brushstrokes of autumn. I made my way to Beeley through hillsides flamed with orange to walk and lunch with long-time friend Brigid. She'd had a difficult year: Covid separating her from her children, a hip and knee problem that had stopped her from driving and walking for a time, and a recent diagnosis of breast cancer. The mammogram had caught the cancer early and the tumour was quickly removed followed by a quick blast of radiotherapy – *just to be sure*.

We wandered up Brookside, the stream babbling alongside the lane. Cottages painted in the signature Chatsworth Estate blue were adorned with pumpkins. Drystone walls and clipped hedgerows funnelled us up toward wood and moor. The larches had taken on the colour of spice.

Brigid and I stopped at the entrance to a farmhouse below the hillside, then retraced our steps to the Old Smithy in the village. We ate pumpkin soup outside in the sunshine and warmed up on hot coffee. We tucked into our sweets, the taste of berry and cinnamon jam a burst of flavour on my tongue, accompanied by oven-crusted scones and cream. We tried not to be distracted by news of the American election on our smartphones, but it was difficult to resist an occasional peep.

'My dad knew Joe and Jill Biden,' Brigid said. 'He phoned home from the States once and said, "Hey, you'll never guess; I'm on the old Air Force One with Joe Biden." My mum didn't believe him. Dad put Joe on. "Joe Biden here. It's true."'

Here in this quintessential English estate village, a place of bucolic sleepiness with names like Brookside, School, Church and Pig Lane, the American election, with all its anger and frustrations, felt very far away. As I drove away, I realised I was privileged in my friendships. In the darker days of winter, they shone a light.

Gossamer

In all things of nature there is something of the marvellous.
– Aristotle

The world shrank and shrank again. I felt trapped. I felt suffocated. I'd had enough of Covid. My positive feelings towards the returning winter had drained away in the morning's fog, the town smothered by cloud, ghosted away.

Sometimes, I felt like that too – a ghost of winter. There was a feeling of being a shadow of myself, flimsy and ethereal, not quite solid. It was a feeling that came with a detachment I sometimes felt in the bookended months of the year: drowsy, dozy, disengaged.

I flung on clothes and tied my boot laces in angry double knots. Was it always going to be like this? One step forward, two steps back? I dragged myself to the car, not wanting to go out. Resisting, resisting, resisting. I felt self-loathing for back-sliding. It was always the same: a reluctance to go out in winter, then the hug of the natural world saying *There, there, feel my embrace. Bathe your senses in my scents and sounds. Feel my healing. I am here for you.* That day, starting out so badly in the muffled, rubbed-out valley, was about to offer me a gift from the mists; something minuscule in the world of nature that would expand the world exponentially with its beauty.

That day, Tom and I returned to Winster to walk the boundaries of the Peak District and Covid lockdown, the village and the Limestone Way lost in fog. As we climbed up to Wyns Tor, the light was pale and translucent, the ground frosted. The White Peak was veiled in radiant white except for the dark lumps of rocks and skeletal trunks and branches of trees that edged a cairn – and the silhouette of Tom in the fog above me. We were trailing in the wake of writer and natural scientist, Llewellynn Jewitt. One winter's day in 1867, he climbed Miss Cresswell's field, near Wyns Tor, and opened a barrow to find fragments of charred bone, charcoal, flint flakes, an iron awl and rivet and decayed wood. He had found the remains of a Bronze Age burial mound, the site of a funeral pyre. Walking Occupation Way above the cairn, the earth of the lane and its central line of tufted grass on the limestone ridge swallowed by fog, it wasn't hard to imagine the world of the Bronze Age people so closely bound with the natural world.

Here, we were wrapped in cloud. Swaddled. Cradled. It felt comforting and *unheimlich* – uncanny – at the same time. Something shifted in my brain, and the anger and frustration I'd felt at home slipped away. On the crest of the ridge, we burst through the inversion mist and out into the blue. Below us, cloud poured through the valley, a river of white. We continued to Bonsall along farm tracks and through the geometry of stone walls punctuated with field barns. Our hearts sang and our chatter filled the air along with a robin's. Above the village, we snaked through a field of hills and holes, a scrubby meadow of old mine-working. We weaved through abandoned rakes where rock plunges into the bowels of the earth. In spring and summer, I'd walked these fields, the ground stitched with rare orchids of curious names: bee, fly and frog. I'd followed paths between Monet-dappled wildflowers: rock rose, wild pansies, violets, yellow rattle, bird's-foot trefoil and harebells. The air surrounding them had been busy with the hum of insects and darting of butterflies.

Now there was just the beige of winter vegetation crusted in pearly white, a familiar November scene – until, that is, we walked into a world so enchanting and otherworldly we couldn't make sense of it to begin with. The ground at our feet had become fluid, a silvery white earth rippling towards us in rivulets – as if we had found ourselves on the banks of a fairy-tale river of light. How could this be? We stood there stock-still, mesmerised by this ephemeral world, until we finally grasped what we were seeing was the creation of tiny money spiders. How delicate the gossamer looked with its fine silky threads dancing across the upland field. The science behind the magic, I later learned, is even more dazzling. The 'sheet weaver' climbs as high as it can, raises a leg, belly pointed heavenward – a phenomenon called tiptoeing – then shoots fine silk threads from its spinnerets into the air. When the elevated silk catches the wind, the spider rides air currents high above the earth, the finely woven web acting as its parachute. And so, this tiny wingless creature, weighing no more than 100 milligrams, surfs the air – ballooning or kiting.

Here in the White Peak, surrounded by the greys of winter, the glowing light of the Inversion mists and the glistening threads of gossamer were lifting my soul. I was flying high like the money spiders.

Patterns on the Shore

The ocean is a mighty harmonist.
– William Wordsworth

At the beginning of the first lockdown, I'd been at peace, cradled in the folds of the Derbyshire uplands. That spring, my home had been a safe place where I could hide from an invisible enemy, but as time went on, I yearned for the coast. It became an obsession. When the government gave us permission to travel as far as we wanted within a day's reach, a friend shared an image of a Lincolnshire 'desert' – a seashore that stretched *ad infinitum* to a block of burnt blue. And emptiness. I needed to go.

The place was Rimac Nature Reserve on the Lincolnshire coast. We'd followed a path through dunes laced with bird's-foot trefoil and orchid to the sea. There had been summer stillness: the small sound of bee, the silent lift of butterfly wings. White admirals, common blues and peacocks fluttered through the air like leaf litter. We'd curved the path between dune and shore, the call of cuckoo following us from somewhere beyond the sea buckthorn. Joy surged unexpectedly. I held onto Tom, the freedom of the shoreline hitting me like a down-in-one – dizzying, intoxicating. I was drunk on ozone, drunk on possibility. The world beyond my island lay just over the blue. The hills that had held me through lockdown had lost their grip. I wanted to reach out beyond my sight line.

'Smell the sea, Tom! Listen, the cuckoo...and the skylark!'

I tightened my grip on his arm and watched the small brown bird hover high above the saltmarsh before dropping to its nest like a plumb bob. Quick as a flash, now you see me, now you don't, tumbling body, tumbling birdsong, athlete of wing and throat. Sweet sound of summer. We reached the beach beyond the marshes, though the shoreline still lay quarter of a mile away. The nearest humans were Lowry stick figures, dark flecks against the bright ocean. In front of us, samphire pushed through sand, the maritime plant once used for making glass, now popular with haute cuisine restaurants. I bit into a fleshy leaf, tasting brine, tasting the sea. We foraged a crop then ran to the shore. I flung off socks and shoes, dipping my feet in icy water, taking a sharp breath against its chill. I felt the rush of blood through my veins and the surge of undertow. Home again, I'd made a potato salad mixed with crisp, salty samphire.

I'd hold onto the flavour of Rimac, carry it through the cold season. But with the second lockdown in November, the taste of samphire was already a distant memory. Still, I remembered Rimac. What was it like on the edge of the ocean on the edge of winter? The wind a cold whip? The sun struggling to make its presence felt? The cuckoo would have long departed to overwinter in Africa. The sea lavender that had spread purple in the fullness of summer would have died away. The acrobatic skylark had no reason to show off.

I remembered the interplay of light on the Taf Estuary in Wales. The North Sea would surely re-energise me just as it had done in Wales, maybe even more so. Now here, on the edge of winter, on the edge of the North Sea, back at Rimac, I discovered the nature reserve had a different canvas to offer. The berries of the sea buckthorn were a dazzle orange in the low light, haws the colour of Christmas. The yellow sky of winter hung low on the coastal hinterland. The sea pale and all aglitter in the other direction.

We set out across the marshes towards Saltfleet Haven, the sun the gentlest of warmth on my back. Saltfleet had been a thriving port in the 1400s, busy with traders, boats and cargo. Fish, salt, bales of wool and grain were all shipped out to the Low Countries. The creek was awash with money – legal and illegal. Now, it was mainly the domain of waterbirds.

We thought we'd follow the creek to the sea. Foolish, foolish! Water channels fan out across coastal wetlands – everyone knows that. Rimac was no exception. Soon, we came to a second creek, forcing us to retrace our steps. I followed the redshanks as they flew low along the creek, razor-sharp beaks and blood orange legs bright against the pale water, the sound of their piping filling the sky.

It took us three hours to reach the sea that day with a picnic interlude, waves gently breaking on the shoreface. I combed the beach for shells: banded wedges, blunt gapers, cockles, silvered oysters, piddocks and razor clams, and filled my fleece pockets. The search concentrated my mind on the treasures at my feet. I was lost in the detail of the shoreline. Lost too in the lullaby of the ocean. My mind was in the present, where it belonged.

'Look, Tom. It feels like we're inside a dome.' I whirled around. The expanse of heaven was all encompassing, sea *and* sky at my feet. The winter blue dropped to meet 360 degrees of coastal edge: ocean, beach, tidal pools, marsh, shrubs and dunes.

We slapped through the shallows, oozing through muddy sand, the samphire now brown and dead and strangled by weed. This was not a lifeless landscape, however. The sea had left ripples across the sand. The wind had sliced across them, creating patterns like tyre tracks. Closer to the back-shore, the wet sand was marked with the crisscross of bird footprints.

'Why are we drawn to patterns in nature?' I asked Tom.

'It's not just patterns, though: it's colours and shapes as well. It's in our DNA from our hunter-gatherer ancestors who had to learn to read the landscape to find food.'

'But there's something about pattern,' I persisted. 'It's the patterns on this walk that jump out at me – the lines on the creek's mud banks, the symmetry of the teasel seed heads on the marshes earlier and these repeating pattern of ripples in the sand. The birds' footprints too.'

As we headed back towards the saltmarsh, the sun flooding the tidal waters with glaring light, I continued to ponder our attraction to pattern. Perhaps it's order in nature that appeals to our rational selves. We see beauty in pattern. We imitate it in art and design. Maybe it stems from our need to find order in the chaos of nature; indeed, in the chaos of the human world.

We followed the sun and its path of silver across the sands, feeling small in the blue of sea and sky. Red poppies painted on rocks brightened a rusting wartime tank. Back on the marshland path, I tuned into the small winter sounds of dunnock, meadow pipit and reed bunting. And once, briefly, the subdued gurgling of a single skylark in the marsh. The songbirds opened my heart. Overhead, a flock of geese, chattering noisily, spread out in V formation across the sky. Their wildness spoke to my soul. My heart lurched.

As we drove home, the pale yellow on the horizon turned faint pink. Blue gave way to twilight white. Across the Atlantic, a man was seemingly flirting with a coup. America was reeling. Their world was turning on its head. New words and phrases were light on tongues: cognitive dissonance, fake news, gaslighting, disinformation, alternative facts, post-truth. Confusion. Winter anxiety had been compounded by my existential anxiety. In the morning, I spent hours scrolling through my phone, curtains closed against the precious light. I was reluctant to get up, loathing myself for my newsfeed fixation. I worried about climate change, world-wide floods and harvest failures, the rage against migration, populism, extreme politics, wars, even fears of WWIII. The list was endless. I scrolled through hundreds of comments too, a toxic place where angry people shouted at each other while holding their ears, metaphorically speaking. At times, I felt angry too. Mostly, I felt helpless. My phone scrolling was an unhealthy habit: I tried to reign it in, but usually failed. Then the self-loathing set in again. It was a vicious circle. Going outside, phone forgotten, was a much-needed respite from my anxious state of mind. For a few hours, I could forget a world at war with itself and lose myself in the here and now.

That mid-November day, I drew from the energy of the ocean, the light-filled sea and sandy shallows. And I realised winter didn't need to be my enemy. Unlike my mobile phone, it was increasingly becoming my friend.

Frost and Fruit Cake

The poetry of the earth is never dead.
– John Keats

The month of November marched on, stamping its feet and making its presence felt. November is the extrovert of the calendar – larger than life and full of drama. It upstages October with its riot of hot colour and bursts of wintry breath. It whips up leaves then slams them down. It strips trees, bleaches and blackens the Peak by turn. Each year, it conjures up inversion clouds and magics away my town in the valley. Our castle on the skyline is there one moment, gone the next. Masson Hill is frequently covered in the white sheet of fog, the magician of winter ready for the big reveal. There are days when the moorland above town is bright with sunshine, the sky clear, while down on the valley floor everything is dusky dark and shadowy. In the upside-down world of our mist-shrouded town, rainfall feels fragile and light. Towards the end of the month, the magician of winter, turned graffiti artist, sprays the Peak District silver and washes moorland and meadow in ice-cream mint.

As November 2020 came to an end, the temperature hovered just above zero. I dug out woollen tights and my down jacket and drove through the cloud inversion to Alport where the rivers of Lathkill and Bradford converge just inside the Peak Park. Early morning was always the most difficult time of day: the struggle to reach beyond the darkness, the temptation to cocoon in the duvet and withdraw from the world. I was so slow to emerge from the darkness into the light that I missed the best part of the day when the light was soft and full of promise. I was going to change this: the first light of day was the sweetest.

I set out along the Lathkill, the ground hard with frost, the river steaming, hills sugared. Grass crackled underfoot. I followed the hedgerow that separated me from the river, small birds darting through twigs. I reached Raper Lodge, used in an adaptation of D.H. Lawrence's *The Virgin and the Gypsy*. Across the river, a little fishing hut stood on the bank, ravens circling the woodlands above it, black on white, their cries harsh on the air. At the lane, I turned right to stand on the packhorse footbridge; the weir on the Lathkill smoking; mallards, bottoms-up, searching for food. I headed up the woodland path. Where the fence ended abruptly, signs warned against trespassing. I dared to cross over to the fishing hut and peered in through the window to see a large fishing net propped against the wall. Mugs lined a shelf with lanterns. I didn't linger, knowing I was committing a small act of disobedience. I slunk back to the path and climbed the lane to Youlgreave, dropping down through steep woodland to follow the River Bradford now back to Alport. White limestone cliffs and fields of frost contrasted the black of curly-horned Balwen Welsh mountain sheep. Winter could be enchanting, I realised with surprise.

Back in the warmth of the house, I wanted sugar — sugar and butter and eggs, flour and sweet syrupy fruit. I wanted the food of winter. Didn't our ancestors gorge on the fruits of the autumn harvest, storing up fat reserves for the barren winter months ahead? I'd make a boiled cake. I measured out two cups of dried fruit and boiled the fruit in water with sugar, butter, cinnamon and grated nutmeg until it became thick and syrupy. I sieved the flour and bicarbonate of soda and cracked open two eggs. I folded the boiled fruit with the flour and the beaten eggs over and over until the white of flour no longer showed through the creamy brown mix, then tipped the mixture into the cake tin. The rhythmic folding, the warmth of the kitchen, the smell of spice and fruit from the oven, the riverside ramble, they had all helped to take away the dread of winter. My cheeks flamed from the heat of the oven after the frosted walk.

I had recoiled in the cold and dark, but I had made myself do it. The rivers, meadows, woodlands and uplands, sparkling in frost and softened by the first light of day, had shown me another narrative. I'd returned home full of light and energy.

Steaming Soups and Sizzling Stews

I live on good soup, not on fine words.
– Molière

As November closed, fiery leaves giving way to bones of trees, the fog moved in semi-permanently, lying low in our town, clawing hilltops and valley sides. Light drizzle turned to heavy showers. Rain rattled the window. It was time to light the wood burner and fill the house with the glow of lamps and candles and the smell of winter vegetable stews and smoking logs. *Hygge* is claimed by the Danes, but the language of winter comfort exists in all its different forms across northern Europe, where cold and dark bookend the year: *Kos* in Norwegian, *Gemütlichkeit* in Germany; *Gezelligheid* in the Netherlands, and in Scots dialect the phrase to *coorie up*, expressing the most essential of human comforts – cosying up to someone you love. Tom was my winter comfort.

The *Gemütlichkeit* of the German-speaking world was one I knew well. I'd spent a winter in the Swiss Engadine in an Alpine house of wood panelled walls, log-warmed rooms and a large picture window that brought the outdoors in. We'd arrived late autumn at Silvaplanersee and watched the lake freeze over, burbling and popping, growling and rumbling as liquid turned to solid ice. When the first snows arrived, they didn't stop. Paths were cleared, the walls of snow growing higher until I couldn't see over the top. The layer of ice on Silvaplanersee was covered in snow, only the flatness of its surface indicating that a body of water had once existed in its place. I spent days cross-country skiing across the frozen lakes of Silvaplana and Sils, where the land dropped away to Italy at Maloja. Sometimes I turned right and skied across Lej da Champfèr and St Moritzersee. Once, I skied all the way to Zuoz in the wild Lower Engadine – a *skimarathon* length – where villages of painted gables gave way to forest, untamed river and boulder.

Later, my love of the Graubünden mountains was replaced by the flatlands of the Netherlands and its big skies. We mostly sailed there on the edges of winter – November or February. We cycled the polders and the North Sea islands, the wind slicing through our bodies, cold needling our faces, toes and fingertips numb. But there was always a café with blankets and candles, low lights, fire and *appeltaart* warm from the oven. And in the wooden beach cafés that hadn't been dismantled for winter, you could rest up and storm-watch. And I learned from end-of-year trips to Scotland, the further north you travel in winter, the more compressed the light is – more lustrous and brilliant. Startling, even. In the Highlands, I found winter when the rest of the island was damp and grey. Mountains were covered in snow, or at least sugared in frost and ice. In Derbyshire, my hills are small – more upland plateau – and snow a rarity, but I recreated continental *Gemütlichkeit* with my log burner and candles. After a week of walking coast, woodland and meadow, we hunkered down on a day of drizzle. I served up strong coffee and cinnamon-spiced *Lebkuchen* and dreamed of Switzerland. Food isn't just nourishment, it's also memory. In the kitchen, I braised meat, added potatoes, carrots and stock, the vegetables smothered in ground black pepper and finally onion, softened until translucent and still full of flavour. We ate the Irish stew by the fire. This was the food of my Irish childhood – days spent in a County Armagh of soft rains, the aroma of burning peat mingling with the fat of meat.

In English, we talk about homesickness to express our longing for home; in German, the simple compound word is *Heimweh*. *Fernweh*, the antonym to *Heimweh*, turns the idea of homesickness on its head. The word can be traced back to Prince Hermann Ludwig Heinrich von Pückler-Muskau, not the punchiest of names, but certainly one that leaves you in no doubt of his standing. In his book of 1837, *The Penultimate Course of the World of Semilasso: Dream and Waking*, the prince coined the word *Fernweh* while pondering his travels, explaining he had never suffered from homesickness but rather from 'away-sickness'. In Covid lockdown, the sense of *Fernweh* was heightened for me. Late spring, I longed for the sea, not that far from where I lived, yet impossibly far away because it was out of bounds. By late summer, I could visit the sea, but I yearned to go beyond the shores of my island across the North Sea to mainland Europe. Towards the end of the year, locked down again, the yearning for places of hard winters and deep snow became intense. The short afternoon of wet snow I'd experienced a few days previously above the snow line of my town in Farley Wood had filled me with an ache for my long-ago home in the Engadine of Switzerland.

But here I was in England, the rain doing a horizontal dance across the valley, the sparrows leaving the shelter of the hedgerow across from my house to bathe in a road puddle. In winter, there is solace in memory. In winter, there is solace in food. On those days when the rain feels too relentless to venture outside, the two together were an antidote to my winter blues.

All those years ago in the Graubünden, I had often set out to ski across the frozen and snow-covered lakes. The air stabbed my throat with its iciness, pricked my cheeks with needles of cold. The mountain valley smelled of snow – not really a smell at all but a sensation of purity – along with pine and woodsmoke. The minus temperatures and the exertion of pushing down on my skis had been exhilarating as I'd sped along the valley floor. There had been quietness except for the occasional boom of an avalanche, the muffled hum of distant traffic and the swish of my skis. Occasionally, I'd stopped at one of the mountain inns in Maloja or Sils or further away in the wilder Lower Engadine for a bowl of *Bündner Gerstensuppe* – a Graubünden broth made with barley, winter vegetables and Bündnerfleish, locally cured beef. The inns in those mountain villages of steeply pitched roofs, painted gables and wide, arched wooden doors, tempted me in with their aroma of spiced sausage or potato-crisped *rösti*. And I knew it would be warm inside. The dining rooms were rustic with slabbed stone floors, heavy wooden tables and chairs and carved chandeliers. The beaded eyes of stuffed deer heads stared down from walls, making me glad I wasn't eating the local venison. The sounds in the dining rooms were as minimal as those in the muffled valley – just the scrape of chair on stone, or the bare bones of conversation that emitted from dour mountain folk speaking in an ancient Latin tongue that had been stranded in this remote mountain valley. But the Bündner *Gerstensuppe* was unrestrained, thick, creamy and filling, and served up with great slabs of bread.

I had never cooked *Gerstensuppe* myself but on that English Sunday of rain and memories, I impulsively decided to try it. I found a recipe online and sifted through my cupboards and the fridge for the ingredients. I lacked the main ingredient, *Bündnerfleish*, but I had everything else: spice, bay leaves, onions, garlic, carrots, leek, celery, potatoes, parsley, stock and cream – and an alternative to cured beef I found in another recipe: *Speckwürfeln*, cubes of fatty bacon. And so, I sat in front of the wood burner and tasted the mountains, tasted my past.

December

On a Snowy Evening

The woods are lovely, dark and deep.
– Robert Frost

The first snow fell on the 4th of December, hesitantly, half-heartedly. It came down wet, disappearing into the warm earth. But up on Masson Hill – above our snow line, where the temperature is often a degree or two colder – it was beginning to cover its higher reaches, and soon there was a stripe of Nordic winter white above a lower stripe of damp-island green.

If the snow wouldn't come to me, in my three-degree valley, I would go to it. I pulled on boots and climbed the hill behind me to Farley Wood. I entered Narnia, not through a wardrobe, but through a muddy tree-lined track between green meadows. In the plantation, there was no frozen snow, carol-deep and crisp and even. Warm feet had rubbed away the thin layer of soft, wet snow, leaving a trail of footprints on the forest track. In places where the conifers had made an arch over the pathway, the ground was still brown and covered with pine needles, but the trees shivered in silver, and barks and trunks were sketched chalk on charcoal. And there was still the crunch of my boots on snow as I walked deeper into the forest – a sound I loved. The sound of memory and Silvaplanersee.

Other than my feet on the snow, there was stillness. The pines and forest understory that had rung with birdsong back in spring were quiet. There was a brief movement from a small brown bird – a wren, perhaps – in the periphery of my eye. There was a flash of robin red, a flutter in a bush and a faint chirp from somewhere deep within, winter thin. Then silence again.

I came across a dog walker, approaching from the opposite direction, and we grinned at each other in delight as if we were the only people who had discovered this half-frozen place above the green valley. 'Isn't it beautiful?' the woman said, and we laughed, the snow making us drunk with happiness.

After a while, I came to a sign attached to a tree that said, 'Joy to the world.' I had felt joy in this quiet forest, in this brightened landscape, re-coloured white and silver. The sign informed me that I was on the Jo Cox Way and my joy spilled into sadness. I read on: *We really enjoyed last year's Christmas baubles up here. So, we invite all walkers to join us in adding socially distanced Christmas decorations to Jo Cox Way over Advent – to affirm community over isolation. We wish everyone a joyful and peaceful Christmas and undiminished New Year.*

Who had started this tradition? I wondered. Forestry England? One of the dog walkers? I carried on, looking for baubles rather than birds. First, I spotted a red one capped in snow and surreally hanging from a birch, then a globe of sky blue and a tangerine orange, shortly followed by a pair, pink and beige, hanging from pine branches. As I walked deeper into the forest, there were no more baubles or dog walkers. When the broad forest track came to an end, I passed a nursery of young conifers on my left, a dry stone wall topped with snow on my right. I wondered if I were to walk far enough, would I reach a road? The forest was not very big, but still I feared I would lose my way, and the light was dimming. I turned around and retraced my steps.

In the gloaming, the forest looked uncanny, foreign to my mild island, but the snow was already on the melt. There was the sound of soft plops as cotton wool balls slid off branches onto the ground. This world, so delicate and fleeting, would be gone by tomorrow. I knew that. How different it had been in the Swiss Engadine, where the snow had lain all winter. When it had finally melted in spring, the green had hurt my eyes after months of monochrome. The colour! It had dazzled in its brightness.

As the light faded out, I stopped to listen. The plantation was still but for the fall of snow from trees. Had the forest emptied of birds? I strained my ears. There was not even the subdued song of a robin or the gloaming *mek-mek-mek* of a blackbird. Once, I thought I caught a glimpse of bird slip into the undergrowth, a flash of brown, too fast to ascertain what it was.

All round me, Christmas trees hung with snow. The mantle of the beeches on the perimeter of the plantation lay on the forest floor, hidden beneath a covering of white. It was easy to identify their smooth green barks, even without their leaves. I touched a trunk and felt its core robustness, felt how it was rooted to the ground. It was waiting, gathering strength before its renewal in spring.

At home, I looked up the science of trees in winter. I learned they go into preservation mode ahead of the season. Deciduous trees drop their leaves, slow down growth or even stop it altogether. Water retention is reduced, minimising the risk of ice crystals penetrating the wood and damaging cells.

Trees increase the amount of sugar in their branches and root systems, creating their very own antifreeze. In doing so, the freezing point of water and sap is lowered, preventing crystals from forming properly. Dropping leaves doesn't just enable deciduous trees to hibernate, it also means they cope better with winter storms and heavy snows. Able to bend and flex in high winds, they are less likely to be damaged by the weight of snow across a large canopy of leaf cover. While evergreens retain their needles, they too fill their cells with a concentrated sugar solution that also acts as an antifreeze, and like deciduous trees, they reduce the amount of water absorbed in the wood. The science of nature, I realised, was a thing of wonder.

Only the winter's dark nights and cold weather slow us down...a gift from nature? I remembered the words of the British winter lover. I was continuing to rewrite the narrative: winter was not a metaphor for death; winter was a time of resting. I needed to be in harmony with nature's slowdown and recuperate. I needed to draw up to the fire, reflect and acknowledge the source of my fears and anxiety, including the debilitating effects of Covid, and find ways to draw strength in readiness of spring and summer's renewal.

Winter Solstice Among the Stones

Tout change, même la pierre. (Everything changes, even stone.)
– Claude Monet

We set out for Stanton Moor as the light slipped away. This area is riddled with stones. We passed Robin Hood's Stride in the gathering dusk, a heap of stones on the hillside –

two towering columns of rock at either end of the outcrop – over which Robin Hood had allegedly leapt. I preferred the outcrop's other name: Mock Beggar Hall. Tonight, it looked particularly atmospheric against the paling sky, like a Gothic ruin rising out of the hillside. Out of sight, behind the outcrop, there's a standing stone and stone circle. It's a place I've explored over the years. Nine Stones Close – only four in evidence – sits on the crest of an upland meadow. I'd gone there on crisp winter's days, the ground frosted, the stones glistening, the valley sugared; a farmer's trailer parked surreally in the centre of the ancient monument. Below Mock Beggar Hall, there is another outcrop: Cratcliff Tor. Behind fencing, at the base of the tor, there's an alcove and cross carved out of gritstone. This is said to be a Hermit's 'cave', the raised stone slab beneath the overhang an unforgiving but dry bed.

As we drove past, I realised I mostly walked this countryside surrounding Birchover in the depths of winter, when the rain spreads across the hills or the land is bright with sharp winter light. The ancient Derbyshire Portway cuts across this hillside, linking Mam Tor in the Dark Peak with Hemlock Stone near Nottingham. The hermit, Haddon Hall records indicate, once rescued lost travellers from the Derbyshire Portway, a path that had carried the feet of men and women from the Bronze Age to the Middle Ages before falling out of use. He'd guided them down to the medieval castle in the valley below, where 'Ye Old Hermitte' was paid fourpence.

I'd brought my Swiss friend Manuela here with her two sons, Gian and Aurelio. We had scrambled over the rocks of Robin Hood's Stride and hunted out the hermit's cave. Gian loved the rain – holding his face up to the mizzle, running down the hill, arms outstretched, whooping and grinning as water ran down his face. I thought back to my childhood in Northern Ireland when it seemed to rain perpetually. I'd never liked the rain, but if I were to grow to love winters on my island, I had to learn to love wet weather, go out in it. After all, I lived on the edge of Europe where the Atlantic meets the North Sea. I had no choice: these were the days we mainly inhabit.

Still, most weeks I waited out the rain, heading out into the countryside when the grey lid lifted and the clouds parted to reveal a sky of Wedgewood Blue. I knew it wasn't enough. If grey and rain made up the bulk of our winter days, I would have to rewrite that narrative inside my head too. I noted it in my journal.

As our car headlights caught the cliff face of Cratcliff Tor, I imagined the hermit out trapping rabbits in sub-zero temperatures. I imagined him bent over twigs and leaves, blowing life into snow-dampened wood, desperate for the heat of the fire and energy of cooked meat. I imagined him lying on the cold stone slab beneath the damp overhang, his body covered in the skins of animals. There must have been times of famine and feast for the hermit. In a good year, he'd catch a surplus of rabbits. Once, he'd delivered ten of them to Haddon – recorded in the kitchen accounts of 1549. I tried to imagine what it was like for the hermit to survive the dark days either side of the Winter Solstice, at a time when Britain was experiencing a Little Ice Age that had endured from the 15th to the 19th century. How was it for him under the iron grip of winter when rabbits refused to stray from their holes and foxes from their dens, and deer retreated deeper into the woods?

Here in the 21st century, my country was on edge. London and the south-east had gone into full lockdown. Families were told not to travel outside Tier 4 (where you could only travel further afield for work) for Christmas gatherings. Londoners streamed out of the capital to reach family, friends and lovers across the country before the midnight deadline. Lorry drivers were stranded on either side of the English Channel as the French refused entry in the face of a new virulent strain that had originated in the south-east. Food stores promised there was enough surplus food to last for a few days at least. There was anger and frustration. We were used to being in control of our lives. We were used to freedom of choice. If we had enough money, we could travel where we wanted. We could eat exotic food from across the world whatever the time of year. Potentially no more. We had lost the skills of hunting and foraging – and we had no hermit to deliver us a bag of rabbits. Mostly, we didn't know what sacrifice felt like. We didn't know what it was like to live in isolation, outdoors and exposed to the elements. Life in the 21st century was comfortable. On our island, winters were mild, temperatures mostly hovering between 3 and 10 degrees. Food and drink, heat and warmth, easy travel and gatherings across long distances were something many of us took for granted, especially at Christmas. Then Covid arrived.

I turned sharp right onto the road that rises to Birchover. As the road bent left into the village, we passed the Druid's Inn. Behind it, there's another rocky outcrop, its stones carved into seats, staircases, rooms and alcoves by a playful Victorian vicar. But there are much older carvings that appeared to be rock art: a zigzag line possibly representing a snake; touching curves, the petals of flowers; cup marks and rings. On the other side of the village, there are more standing stones and circles: Doll Tor and Nine Ladies. We had chosen to celebrate the turning of the year at Nine Ladies Stone Circle high on the moorland above our valley.

We crossed the moors, a windswept place of bent spindly birches, strangely weathered rocks and slabs of quarried stones. In the valley below, the lights of Darley Dale and Matlock strung out across Derwent Valley, reminding us we were not far away from civilisation. The light was fading out, but as we walked through the heather and bracken our eyes grew accustomed to the gloaming. We plunged into birches, where lights blinked among pale trunks. We were not alone. As we emerged at the Nine Ladies in the woodland clearing, the centre of the stone circle was crowded with New Age Pagans. Children ran through the stone circle, trailing light from their fire brands. Adults huddled in groups with mulled wine. The sweet and fusty aroma of incense – maybe weed – wafted through the air. Smoke curled into an ink-navy sky from fire-pits.

This early Bronze Age monument had seemed the right place to celebrate the shortest day of the year. Our ancestors had erected circles of stones to celebrate the circular nature of life: birth and death, the moon orbiting our planet, the world orbiting the Sun, the changing of the seasons, the lengthening and shortening of the days; the Earth spinning on its axis, its present tilt giving us winter. But from now on in, the days would lengthen again; a promise of spring. Paganism and Christianity had blurred over the centuries. Christianity claimed the Pagan site for itself, giving The Nine Ladies a moral spin: the women frozen for dancing on the Sabbath. It was a Derbyshire version of the biblical wife of Lot, who had been turned into a pillar of salt for looking back at a sinful Sodom. We reached the King Stone that sits outside the stone circle – the Ladies' Fiddler – and felt conscious we were outsiders breaking into the gathering of modern-day Pagans. This wasn't the place for us to mark the shortest day of the year.

We slipped across the moors and stopped on the gritstone path away from the crowd, in the stillness of the moorland edge. The night had fallen, the streetlights smudged in the foggy valley below. The air held moisture from the clouds. We had been told there was a chance of witnessing the 'Star of Bethlehem' for the first time since 1623 – well, realistically 1226, when the stars were last visible to the naked eye under the darkness of night. The Star of Bethlehem, it was suggested, was not one star but two: Jupiter and Saturn perfectly aligned to appear as one intensely bright light. Was this the star – or stars – the three wise men had witnessed in the search for baby Jesus, as the German astronomer Johannes Kepler suggested in 1614? Or had the Star of Bethlehem been an even more unlikely conjunction of three planets – Jupiter, Saturn and Venus – as other astronomers suggested?

Either way, there was no Star of Bethlehem to guide us over the Derbyshire moors in the Winter Solstice of 2020. But we'd witnessed a near alignment the previous night when we'd gone outside our front door, just as the grey of darkness began to eke through a primrose sky. And in that moment, a band of cloud stepped aside to reveal a sliver of moon, and just to its right the planet of Saturn hovering above Jupiter, almost touching – something I would never witness again. I felt my heart thrill. The light in the dark was a revelation.

The darkest nights were on the turn and, as with the winter, I was learning to love their gifts.

Jólabókaflóð – The Christmas Book Flood

Blindur er Bóklaus Maður. (Blind is a bookless man.)
– Icelandic saying

Tom and I had visited Iceland at the end of summer, their September already on the cusp of winter. I had loved this otherworldly place with its thrashing seas, its bright light, black sands, great columns of basalt, receding glaciers and ice caps, and seas of floating ice. This was a landscape unlike any other I'd ever experienced. The strangeness of its topography was reflected in the language of its volcanoes that my geologist used to describe it. *Pahoehoe* was the ropey lava that formed the basalt at Þingvellir. *Paw-hoey-hoey* was bubble gum on my tongue, a word to roll around the mouth. *Aa* described the broken and rubbly basalt. *Ah-ah, ah-ah.* I repeated it like a small child, delighting in its echolalia. As we drove the coast between Dyrhólaey and Jökulsárlón, we passed *tuyas*, the angular flat-topped, sheer-sided volcanoes that rise from the tundra, and, in contrast, hills so perfectly rounded they looked artificial. This island was wild and inhospitable, and the wind so fierce it almost took the doors off our rented campervan. I couldn't imagine what it would be like to inhabit this place in winter.

That September, I discovered Icelanders celebrate Christmas in the unique way of an island on the edge of the Atlantic. On Christmas Eve, the islanders gift each other a book and settle down to read the evening away. It's not such an old tradition, only dating back to World War II when paper was one of the few commodities that hadn't been rationed. I liked the Icelandic idea of gifting books.

On Christmas Eve, Tom and I set out to climb Matlock
Bank with a bag full of books wrapped in brown paper, a
bright Vanity Fair postcard slipped under parcel string. There
was no Icelandic snow and ice: rain streamed down the steep
pavement; the roads lacquered with rain. We reached my
sister Carrie's house, opened her door and slid the books
across the hallway and crept away. We climbed higher to
Sue's terraced house, pushing her Icelandic gift through
the letterbox, and continued up the Bank. The black streets
reflected the fairy lights of outside decorations: golds, silvers
and the reds and greens of the season. Lights hung under
eaves, adorning window frames and doors, brightening trees
and bushes. We headed down the dark driveway that rolled
down to Gill's kitchen. I could see her form through the
steamed-up window. Gill, on her island house, adrift in the
grounds of a grand villa. A rising tide of new estate houses
on the other side were now threatening to engulf her home. I
could see Gill was spooked by my knocking: she was expect-
ing no one, especially not in lockdown, not on this dark, wet
evening. A widow living on her own, Gill moved away from
the door, like a child pretending not to be there. I pressed
my nose against the glass. Gill had been cooking soup with
shitake mushrooms. The stalks of fungi were stacked up in a
little bowl, miso paste at its side. Gill liked to cook Japanese
food; an interest developed when her eldest son married a
Japanese concert pianist. I called Gill's name, and still uncertain she inched opened the door with fear in her eyes. We
laughed and I handed her the book, not lingering, unable
to step inside. We dropped down to Brigid and Liam, then
crossed the Bank to Ian and Emma, their books landing
through their letter boxes with a thud.

'Maybe next year, we will do the same,' I said to Tom. 'Only this time we'll be able to step out of the cold and celebrate Christmas and the end of Covid with our friends and family.' I imagined Carrie sharing a spicy mulled wine with us; Sue, one of her homemade sloe gins; Gill, sake – Japanese rice wine; Brigid and Liam, a beer; and Emma and Ian, prosecco. We would be light-headed by the time we got home, warmed by friendship, indoor heating and alcohol. The Covid Christmas could be forgotten, I hoped.

A Snowy Christmas Eve

Ik heb natuur en kunst en poëzie, en als dat niet genoeg is, wat is dan genoeg? (I have nature and art and poetry, and if that is not enough, what is enough?)
– Vincent van Gogh

We had not expected snow, although the temperatures were closing in on zero. We had driven to Hayfield below the Kinder Massif in the expectation of a bright, sunny day. I had given up on wearing my down jacket when out walking. Every time, I felt too hot. I would wear a hat, then remove it. I'd pull off my gloves, my hands too warm. Only I had been stomping through the mild valleys of the White Peak; the Dark Peak is colder, the moors higher.

At the bottom of Snake Path, Tom and I paused to read the memorial sign commemorating the arrest of leading members of the Right to Roam Movement following the Kinder Mass Trespass on 24th April 1932. The working-class Mancunians and Sheffield ramblers had met at the top of

Kinder, shaken hands and descended the path feeling elated, but the police had lain in wait at the bottom. The court ruling that led to the imprisonment of its leaders only lent public sympathy to their cause. The path of protest leading to change – like the rough track the protesters had ascended towards Kinder – is long and rocky, but seventeen years later the National Parks and Access to the Countryside Act opened farmland and estate land to the wider public. And so, because of that raggle-taggle group of lawbreakers, I was able to climb up onto the moorland, the air like shards of ice in my throat, the chilled wind stabbing my face. Derbyshire expanded at my feet. I watched the world open out – as it had done for the protesters – both metaphorically and literally, first Hayfield, then New Mills and finally Manchester, with skyscrapers the protesters could never have imagined.

Higher up, the moors were fiery with winter light, the stalks of heather a fierce red, low-lying shrub taking on a glassy appearance. The moorlands stretched out somewhere between mustard and ginger. The burbling of grouse rose from somewhere within the heather, the moorlands alive with their cackling. We turned a corner and two small wooden, white painted huts with slate roofs came into view, tucked into yellow grasslands. Above the old shooters' cabin with its store, the gritstone escarpment of the Kinder plateau marched across the skyline. It felt like we'd somehow found our way back to the sub-Arctic tundra of Iceland.

There is something about the slow, slow ascent onto higher land and the buffeting winds of winter: it catches '*the heart off-guard and blows it open*', as Seamus Heaney wrote in his poem *Postscript*. He was talking about the coast, but the feeling was similar in the sea of this upland grass. How I felt

Heaney's words on these heights. I could have burst with the joy of this wide-open space. There were no winter blues: there was ginger and mustard and buttery yellow; there were the bruised purples of the sky. There were darts of brilliant white sunlight streaming through. There were pools of silver among blackened peat. I paused to take in the patchwork blanket of moorland rising and falling to a distant horizon, and suddenly I was aware of my smallness, my paltry insignificance in the sweep of Dark Peak. I felt humbled, yet bigger at the same time – for I was connected to all of this. I belonged to its vastness. I was bound to the Earth that ground me. Up here on Kinder, I sensed the slow rhythms of my ancestors over millennia. I too was part of the rhythms of time – the hours, days, weeks, months – and returning seasons, the centuries and millennia. What can there be but winter? It belongs to the circle of life. And I belonged to winter, whether I liked it or not. Indoors, or moving from house to vehicle and back to house again, I lost all sense of my place on this Earth. This world would be my home for just the smallest of moments in the vastness of time, in the turning of the seasons. It was a privilege, I realised. *'You are neither here nor there,'* Seamus Heaney wrote in the same poem. *'A hurry through which known and strange things pass.'* Every single time I gathered myself up to go outside in winter, I'd leave the house with reluctance, and every single time, when I opened myself to the world, my heart would be *blown open* all over again.

By the time we dropped off the hillside to Kinder Reservoir, the sky was an angry black. We crossed a wooden footbridge and found a pile of rocks to sit on for our picnic lunch. And as we bit into our sandwiches, the first snow fell, light and delicate, so gentle and pale in the low light. I felt my heart dance a little with the slivers of flakes. They melted into the warmth of our clothes and skin and disappeared into the ground.

'It's not going to lie,' I said to Tom, but a dusting settled on the rocks and covered the track that skirted the reservoir. The fine flakes caught in the grasses and heather, but the snow was not thick or deep enough to cover the moorland vegetation. Only the path was dusted with snow, a snake of white spread out in front of us. This was as near to a white Christmas we would experience. It was enough in this moment.

I thought of Pieter Bruegel's *Hunter in the Snow*, the hunters on the hillside above the village, the shoulders of both the hunters and their dogs hunched, a single scrawny fox slung on a pole, a landscape frozen and devoid of wildlife except for the waiting ravens. The Little Ice Age was at its height in 1565. Those winter months filled Europeans with dread, bringing hardship and starvation. Charles Dickens had written his stories at the other end of it. He wrote of snow-filled streets and frosted nights. We still cling to the white Christmases Dickens depicted in his *Christmas Carol*. Dickens had spent his earliest years in the coldest decade since 1690. He experienced the stallholders who set up shop on the frozen Thames rent free: The Frost Fair. It is because of him that our Christmas trees are covered in 'frosted' tinsel, outside lights sometimes 'drooping icicles'. Christmas cards depict deep snows, and skies clear and star-filled. These depictions bear no resemblance to our mild, green, overcast winters, muddier from rain than hardened with frost, but we still cling to an idealised version of winter that comes from artists and writers. Here on the Kinder foothills, I settled for the few fine flakes caught in the heather and the white path that gleamed pale in front of us – and the blast of Arctic wind that made me feel alive. Back home, I wrote Van Gogh's words in my gratitude diary: *nature, art and poetry*. On this day, it had been a winter feast.

January

New Year Dawn

The mountains are calling and I must go.
– John Muir

The dawn belongs to the birds. The winter sky, often distilled to a single song, a muted fragment, a warning chirp, was now filled with music. In the pre-dawn – the first chink of light pushing through – the tawny owl's final call of the night came from somewhere higher up the Bank.

Down in the town, the joyous ringing song of a thrush echoed round Imperial Rooms. As we walked through the park, the black of sky was just beginning to ease out. A couple came by with coffees from the 24-hour garage, calling out a New Year greeting. The rubbish disposal man cheered at the tidy park; the New Year's Eve crowds hadn't gathered, as was usual in Crown Square to spill into Hall Leys, our small patch of green by the Derwent. It had been a strange New Year – few fireworks, no revelry down below in the valley. No movable feast with my sister and her neighbours further up the hill. For the first time, the Covid restrictions filled me with complete sadness. And an hour before midnight, as our island drifted away from the anchorage of our continent, I felt, all at once, at sea. But then, some German friends unexpectedly video called me. They were dressed in the finest Agatha Christie garb, having just finished solving a murder. Gentle Henri, who had committed the crime, grinned with glee as he held up the murder weapon. Monika, his wife, had 'riled him with an old lover'. I had spoken the most horrendous German, my tongue clumsy after several glasses of wine, but I was clear-headed enough to see that although my nation had abandoned its political and trade alliance with mainland Europe, I was forever bound to it by a shared history and friendship. No one could legislate against that.

Now, along the river, the water shone bright, the sound of its rush downstream rousing me out of my early morning grogginess. As I climbed High Tor, I looked back at the river and the valley road, snaking in unison, the road a parallel steam of black lacquer in the emerging dawn. Edging the A6 were Lego houses with windows of yellow. Beyond that, the lights of the town winked across the hillside. Tom and I reached the top of High Tor as pewter paled to silver. We skirted round the rakes Patrick and I had explored one summer when the gates had been left open. The Victorians had taken guided parties of tourists through the lead vein, but our council had deemed it unsafe and had secured them with padlocked metal gates at either end. In hard winters, when the ground is thick with snow or frost, the warmer air from the rake steams out of its opening. Not today. Some snow still lay on the upper ground above the Derwent Valley, but the thaw was setting in. Tom and I skidded downhill and re-entered the park. The birds were in full song, cutting across each other like an orchestra warming up: coal tit, robin, wren, blackbird and goldcrest.

This was the way I wanted to start the new year – with gathering light and birdsong.

In Search of Starlings

La richesse que j'atteins vient de la Nature, la source de mon
inspiration. (The richness I achieve comes from nature, the
source of my inspiration.)
– Claude Monet

Conquering winter melancholy isn't always easy. There were days when the lacklustre skies bore down too heavily, the light too mean. And in the winter of 2020-2021, there was the prison of Covid. The new year – that cherished cliché of new beginnings – continued its downward spiral from the dying days of 2020. A new variant of coronavirus was spreading at an alarming rate through the population. We went into a third lockdown. The Mayor of London declared a major incident, the city's hospitals close to being overwhelmed. The death toll surged past 80,000 and at times the UK was listed as the most infected country in the world per capita.

The Earth shrank again. My motivation was as low as the winter light. There were days when the crawl out of bed felt too much. Watching the insurrection of Capitol Hill provided a shameful fascination. Five people were killed. The shining city on the hill – the American 'beacon of hope to the world' – had been tarnished, its offices ransacked, its legislators threatened. The crowd outside called for the lynching of Vice President Pence for not blocking the certification of Biden, the President Elect. The gallows and noose were already in place in front of the Capitol – symbolic or not. The President's son, Donald Trump Junior, surrounded by multiple screens televising the revolt, grinned with glee while his girlfriend danced in excitement. President Trump was rumoured to have watched the unfolding scenes from the safety of the White House mesmerised; this was the 'fight' he had surely hoped for. Once again, I'd failed to reign in my newsfeed obsession. Like Trump, I was fixated by the scenes on Capitol Hill.

So when I finally opened the curtains in my bedroom, the world outside threw me off-kilter. It was not black but washed in pure light. Masson Hill sparkled in frost; the hill-tops of Riber Castle, High Tor and the Black Rocks sugared in misted light. The slate roofs in the valley were gleaming, limestone gables illuminated gold. Our street sparrows flew from bush to bargeboard and bargeboard to bush, their chirps ringing through the air. The murky days of grey mizzle had given way to one of bright crisp cold.

Tom and I drove to Middleton Moor in search of star-lings. This part of the Peak District is scarred with the gaping wounds of blasted rock – great holes in the ground and half-eaten hillsides. When the sites are abandoned, nature moves in and softens naked rock with the creep of moss and lichen. Limestone darkens and rocky craters are filled with water. On Middleton Moor, Lagoon 4 is unceremoniously used to settle limestone slurry. It is also the place where hundreds and thousands of starlings gather to dance in the winter sky.

As I started up the quarry track, a birder was packing away his telescope.

'Seen anything interesting?' I called.

'Nothing. Absolutely nothing. Well, nothing apart from a couple of jackdaws.'

'Two-a-penny jackdaws,' I laughed.

'Two-a-penny indeed. The problem is it's frozen up there and the waders have gone elsewhere.'

'We've come up in the hope of seeing a starling murmuration,' I told him.

'Hmm. Good luck with that. I saw a good display about a month ago. Not sure how it is now. The reedbeds get flattened in the snow and ice and they move to lower land to find a warmer roosting site. It's freezing cold – rather you than me hanging around until dark.'

We walked on, skirting the lagoon along a track of white. Ice crunched underfoot. The sun spilled light through milky pink. We passed a frozen dewpond circled in snow. The black fingers of ash laced through bleached hills. At a second gateway to the flooded quarry, there were no hostile signs. We slipped over the gate and walked down to the water's edge.

Lagoon 4 has been home at times to curlews and cuckoos, sanderlings and sandpipers, wheatears and wagtails, but tonight the water, frozen and half-covered in snow, was devoid of resident and overwintering waterbirds. In contrast, the snowy path we followed around the perimeter of the lagoon revealed the busy traffic of animals: rabbit, fox and the arrowhead footprints of birds, now hidden from sight.

I'd anticipated a harsh landscape of mud and pipes, but instead I found a frozen world of ice-bright beauty. The fiery warmth of reed in the diffused light broke up the black and white of hill and thicket. This was a landscape more akin to the frozen tundra of Siberia, not the soft greens of Peak District upland. On the other side of the lagoon, reedy grass gave way to bulrush, cotton wool buds of snow caught in the poker heads.

We watched two magpies lift and fly across the lagoon but there was no sign of the starlings. Two groups of crows skirted the edge of the water and continued their flight over the frozen water. No starlings would be roosting here on this frosted night. The light dimmed to a low starched white. We rounded the northern head of the lagoon to see the flashing headlights of a cyclist. He climbed the snowbound quarry track before disappearing into the curves of the moorland.

'Coffee?' Tom asked.

I nodded. We stood there enjoying the hot bitter liquid we sweetened with squares of milk chocolate and wrapped ourselves in the absolute stillness of the gathering darkness. On the way back, the cracked ice of puddles caught the blush of sky. The headlights of a farmer's four-wheel drive shone a pool of light across an upland field. The sheepdog and its four-wheeled co-worker gathered sheep across the hillside and guided them to a long trough of winter feed, the vehicle's lights a warm glow on woolly backs.

There had been no spectacular murmuration across the reedbeds – no squeeze and spread, no darkening and lightening, no liquid flow of inky birds across the sky. But we had found, for all of that, an uncanny place of snow and ice that had slipped into the winter-mild of England.

In this world, there was only the now. There was only this place.

The Deerhunter

Adopt the pace of nature. Her secret is patience.
– Ralph Waldo Emerson

The world continued to shrink, the plans I made to visit the coast to seal-watch and storm-watch had to be abandoned.

The government told us not to travel. The daily death toll had gone well beyond the thousand mark. Borders were closed. Grey piled on grey: the grey of sky, the grey of earth; the grey of mood. In spring, when my perimeters had been reduced to a few miles around my home, they had expanded in other ways. Shoots had burst through the earth. Flowers unfurled. Fruit trees blossomed; woodlands swelled with birdsong. The days grew. Sunshine bathed the garden in gentle warmth. But now in this winter lockdown, the world seemed to be shrinking in every way. Days were snap short. The sky leaned low. Nature was muted. Covid was a constant low-level anxiety. It was beginning to creep into my dreams. The government's revised message 'stay alert' reverted to 'stay at home.' But I had to get out. As winter continued, I saw that the outdoors was an antidote to my winter blues, something the Arctic Finns had realised a long time ago.

I dared to drive the just under six miles to Beeley – the Chatsworth Estate village I'd walked with Brigid in autumn. I hid the car under the high wall of the vicarage, nervous of being fined by Derbyshire police for straying from my hometown, even though the government contradicted themselves over what staying local meant. I couldn't travel to the coast to seal-watch, but I could hunt for deer on my doorstep – or at least on the doorstep of the stately Chatsworth House.

From One Arch Bridge at Calton Lees, I tramped up the lane leading to Calton Lees' parkland estate houses, a huddle of stone-built dwellings painted in the signature Chatsworth Blue. The climb up the hill was gentle. My lungs filled with cold air. My heart pumped. My feet found a rhythm. My mind cleared and tuned into my surroundings. The hedgerows were noisy with the chatter of sparrows. I watched them dart through the gaps of twigs. The sound of sparrow was replaced by the burble of brook. It was a light-filled day, the sky a rare winter block of blue. I pushed through a gate and followed the track across a meadow, detouring to a cottage that lay at the bottom of the sloping field. The cabin could have been transported from a Russian folk tale with its intricately carved wood window surrounds and bargeboards and clapboard cladding. It had been modelled on a miniature Russian farmhouse that had been sent to the 6th Duke of Devonshire by the brother of Tsar Nicholas of Russia.

Back on track, I crossed New Piece Wood and out onto open parkland. A long line of fallow deer underscored the bump of escarpment on the skyline above the stately home. I started down the slope towards a clump of oaks, the deer grazing on the other side. They shifted lazily away from me as I came out the other side. I sat on a bench to observe them. They whined softly like puppies. Their behinds looked comically like the eyes of racoons, with their dark tails dividing rumps of white edged in black. Their backs were autumn auburn and spotted winter-snow. The bucks were magnificent with their regal antlers, though one male looked oddly unbalanced with a single antler. I sat for a while watching the deer graze the grass, lost in the present, just me and the deer. No external thoughts. No cluttering of the brain. After a while, I stirred myself and headed around the side of the ha-ha (a sunken ditch used on estate parklands to keep out deer) that circled Edensor. Avoiding the village, I cut down to the Derwent.

The river was full, its weirs spilling a roar of water. A grey heron stood frozen on the far bank, just below the weir. I stopped and watched, willing the waterbird to move. But it remained there, inanimate. Time halted; the parkland condensed to this grey heron I was locked into. I fixed my human eye on its black animal eye, its pupil edged in nuclear yellow. But it seemed indifferent to me, unmoving, focused on the river, its next meal, hoping it would land at its feet. It was a scraggy old thing, its ragged coat hung like a rain-bedraggled cape beneath its long scrawny neck. The heron had the appearance of an old man, shoulders hunched, content in his own company. *Do you see me,* I wondered, *or do you not care I'm eyeballing you on the opposite bank?* I continued to wait, wanting to see it take off over the water, but the heron remained statuesque, as if in a trance. I let my need for something to happen go and fell into the heron's stillness. I felt its patience, its unhurriedness, its contentment just to be. I allowed myself to be the heron for a moment: watching, breathing, being.

After a while, I roused myself, leaving the wader to its solitary world, and carried on to Beeley. I had seen no human on my walk, just the sparrows, deer and grey heron, these creatures oblivious to Covid, knowing only the unhurried turning of day and night, as they had always done. The Chatsworth parkland, devoid of all other human life, had been mine and theirs alone.

I added a note to my winter journal: *Winter's breath is gentler, slower. Reduced. But there's still life. In this winter tapestry, there's beauty in its finely rendered detail. I just have to look.*

The Woodpecker

Mon souhait est de rester toujours comme ça, vivre tranquillement dans un coin de natur. (My wish is to stay always like this, living quietly in a corner of nature.)
– Claude Monet

Tom and I had stumbled on the woodpecker in the spring of the first lockdown. We'd gone to Clough Wood, spilling over with bluebells, the brookside bright with marsh marigold. We'd seen the footprints of melanistic fallow deer – Norwegian blacks – in the mud and hoped to catch a glimpse of the majestic animal with its dark sleek body and pale antlers. I'd read herds of more than 100 roamed Clough Wood. I peered into the trees, but the deer remained elusive. Still, the swathes of bluebells after the grey of winter and the rattle of woodpecker in the thickest part of the wood more than compensated.

The woodpecker is the sole percussionist among the avian songsters, a headbanger and showman drummer. Its performance is energetic, and like all good musicians who invest in the best instruments, the woodpecker seeks out tree trunks producing the loudest and most piercing reverberation. These drumming maestros achieve up to forty beats per second. Humans, in contrast, only achieve half the woodpeckers' speed at best. With so much headbanging, you'd think the bird would live with a perpetual migraine; not so, as the spongy mass between skull and beak protects the bird from brain damage.

Nine months later, in the depths of winter, I wondered if I could find the woodpecker again in Clough Wood. I doubted it, but I set off anyway on a dreich winter's day. The clouds were heavy with rain, just holding off. I passed the remains of an old mining engine house and continued along the path we'd trodden in spring. Instead of bluebells, wizened oak, sycamore and beech leaves covered the ground. Broken branches, smothered in moss, littered the understory. The path that had been bone-dry in April was now a quagmire. I slapped through mud, bracing myself against the slide of slope. The light was dim, the woodland silent. I was the only human in these woods. I tried not to compare the experience to the previous spring when sunlight had spilled through the trees, but failed. My mood was as gloomy as the colour-starved woodland.

But then, something changed. I rounded a corner to see streamlets cascading off the hillside to the brook on the valley floor. On the other side of the stepping stones, I sat down on a moss-covered log, my surroundings softened by the greens of Scots pines and river runoff. I needed to remember to take time to be still, I chided myself. I breathed in slowly, counted, opened my flask and poured a coffee. Still, I fretted the liquid was too hot to drink as quickly as I needed to; the light draining from the sky. I smiled at myself: *Why didn't I just surrender to the moment?* I put my cup down and tuned into the music of the brook and the slow creak of pine in the wind. For a moment, the past and the future faded out. This dank winter woodland had its own beauty. I just needed to give myself up to it. After a while, I tramped on, the coffee warm in my belly, my heart rate slower – the joy of forest bathing in winter. I headed to the spot where I'd heard the woodpecker, and there it was, the rapid rapping on wood again, this time duller, more muted on the wet bark.

I looked up and caught a flash of red, black and white. The great spotted woodpecker! It flew higher into another tree before disappearing into the woodland. I'd come with little expectation but had been rewarded just the same.

I retraced my steps to the car. It began to drizzle. I reached for my hood, then changing my mind, left it down. Water dampened my hair and cheeks. I held my face up to the rain, as Gian had done, yielding to its soft dampness, yielding to the gathering dusk. It felt okay – and then to my surprise, I realised it felt good.

February

Resurrecting a Winter Past

Snow had fallen, snow on snow.
– Christina Rossetti

My eyes adjusted to the dimness of the roof space, chinks of ice-cold air filtering through the gap between the stone wall and eaves. Outside, the ground was covered in a thin layer of snow, but on the moorland above the town, it lay deeper. I started the hunt for the long bag of memories from a snow-bound winter thirty-five years ago. I pushed back camping stoves, tents and a roof box, but it wasn't there. Could I have thrown it out? I crawled into a lower space running behind the smaller attic room, stacked with more boxes of games, toys and books. Then, against the eaves, I felt the stiff fabric of a bag. Carefully, I tugged it out, dragged it onto the landing and unzipped it. Yes, my old cross-country skis were still there along with the beige-handled suede poles. The shoes! Did I still have them? I found them in the wardrobe of the spare room. How had I attached them to the skis? I lifted one foot and slotted the metal hook of the shoe into the bar on my ski. Now for the plastic lever. It had to be clamped down over the metal hook and bar. I pulled and pulled, but the lever wouldn't shut. Intuitively, I bent my foot forward, and click, the lever closed over. Now for the other one. It was difficult to hold my balance as I pulled with all my might. Then they were on. Had it always been this hard? I was out of breath just standing on the landing.

All I had to do now was to remember how to move on them. The skis had lain in the darkness of the attic for more than a decade – and another twenty-four years before that. They had been bought for me by Heidi, my au pair employer in Switzerland. We'd taken them up to her mountain chalet in the Graubünden that winter long ago, driving through isolated hamlets of steeply pitched dwellings high in the Albula Mountains. Even in November, the snow-plastered Albulas were formidable, appearing almost vertical, the snow drifts neck-deep in places. From Lej da Güglia, the road dropped quickly down to Silvaplana, then bridged the half-frozen water to Surlej, my winter home. There in the Upper Engadine, the U-shaped valley floor sits at almost 6,000 feet. Heidi's house was wedged between the lakes of Silvaplana and Champfèr on a rocky hillside bluff surrounded by pines overlooking the water's edge. For four months, I traversed the four Upper Engadine lakes with my skis, stopping for coffee and creamy *Quarktorte* or winter-warming *Gerstensuppe*. That winter, I'd been immensely happy, luxuriating in the bright snow-filled days of the outdoors. I had loved winter in the Alps.

Back in the present, I unclipped the skis again. It was eleven years since I had taken them out in the big freeze of 2009-2010. I'd skied from Cromford to Whatstandwell along the canal, the icy snow-compacted path allowing me to move quickly over the towpath. At Whatstandwell, where I'd waited for the train, strangers had looked at me with my skis slung over my shoulder in curiosity. I'd skied alongside the railway line between Matlock and Darley Bridge too, and back along the River Derwent and onto the town bridge to more bemused looks. But it had been a thrilling experience in the continental-deep snow and brilliant blue skies. After that year, the snow had never fallen long enough or deep enough in the valley for me to repeat the experience, and it hadn't occurred to me to try the forest tracks on top. Until now. Would I remember how to ski? But now the snow had covered the forest floor. I hoped I could rediscover the thrill of winter from all those years ago in the Upper Engadine.

Skiing Through Forest

It is the life of the crystal, the architect of the flake, the fire of the frost, the soul of the sunbeam. This crisp winter air is full of it.
– John Burroughs

The weather forecasters promised temperatures would stay below zero. They promised snow. They promised bright days of blue skies. At first, the sky teased with a fine dusting of snow that drifted across the sky before melting into the earth. Micro hailstones rolled briefly across our garden patio and under the garden furniture before disappearing. We'd found an Arctic world and biting wind on the upland moors, but the valleys below shone emerald. At the beginning of the second week in February, the snow fell harder and the temperature, as promised, stayed firmly below freezing. The rain-flooded Derwent Valley yielded to white. I packed my cross-country skis and sticks into the bag along with a rucksack of snacks and climbed the Bank to Farley Wood high above the town. Walkers looked at me and my ski bag as if I was mad. Perhaps I was! On top, the forest track was completely covered in snow. I clipped on my skis, put the bag in my rucksack and set off. Something clicked. The muscle memory took over. Automatically, I bent my ankles and knees. Automatically, I stretched and glided while my arms and sticks swung in counter-rhythm. Automatically, I pushed forward from the hips. The wood was silent but for the occasional footsteps of approaching dog walkers. I had to concentrate on the ground as here and there gravel poked through the layer of snow. The dog walkers looked at me oddly; it was rare for someone to cross-country ski in Derbyshire. One or two even directed me to a sloping field, failing to understand the long-running nature of *Langlauf*. Once or twice, when I lost concentration, a ski would catch on a small patch of exposed gravel, jerking it to a halt while throwing me forward. My heart thudded then settled. As I skied through the zigzag of forest track, I spent more time shuffling than gliding, but the feeling of slipping – sometimes smoothly – over the earth suited the otherworldliness of this snow-bound forest. The lack of cross-country ski tracks also made my journey difficult. Even the smallest camber on the path caused my skis to slide to one side, but while I didn't dare to look up at the silvered trees, I could tune into the song of a robin, the rattle of a blue tit and the flute of a coal tit.

How different had it been in the Engadine. I'd flown across the lakes, my skis hardly touching the ground. One night towards the end of winter, Heidi suggested a night-time ski. The Alps were bathed in bright moonlight, the snow speckled with ice crystals. We hadn't needed torches, the valley floor shimmering with silver light. The snow was crunch-hard, and the sound of our skis echoed across the frozen lake. We headed for the lights at Maloja. The rhythmic swish-swish of our skis entranced us, along with the star-sequined canopy over our heads and the blue shadows that stretched across the valley. The mountains glowed pale above the dark smudge of forest. Our senses were heightened. Our fingers and toes tingled. Our breath smoked. Our laughter, sharp in the night air, tinkled like shards of ice. All at once, I felt the thrill of existing. I wanted to hold this moment, but it could never be. Spring came with the melt, and we returned over the Julier Pass to Zurich.

Back in England, I skied up a side-track where pines had been felled. Among the churned-up ground, there were poles of white, totem-like – the torsos of trees left standing in isolation. The path was lined with bundles of spindly twigs where the understory of the forest has been cleared. Snowflakes began to drift downwards. Soundless. And I felt the words inside my head were drifting into silence with the snow.

The Joy of Human Connection

When one tugs at a single thing in nature, he finds it
attached to the rest of the world.
_ John Muir

The snow fell again that night. A dusting of icing sugar in the valley, deeper on top. I returned to the forest. At the entrance of Farley Wood, birds gathered as if in welcome. I clipped on my skis, watching blue tits flitter from bush to tree, their songs sweet on the cold air, and set off. The plantation rang with human voices too. Small children in all-in-one suits with red polka-dot cheeks ran after their dogs along the snow-covered path. Couples and family groups shouted excitedly, their words bouncing through the Scots pines and Christmas firs. The brightness of snow and sky had brought the plantation to life. I headed deeper into it. The sky silvered, the forest dimmed, and snow began to fall again. The walkers melted away and I was alone. After a while, the forestry track petered out and I had to turn back. On the main trail again, two strangers called out to me.

'Did you see the deer? They just ran out in front of our path.'

'What were they?' I asked.

The women shook their heads, not sure.

'Fallow deer? Were they spotted?'

They shook their heads again.

'Black Norwegian?' I wondered if they strayed to this side of the valley.

'No, definitely not black.'

'Maybe a muntjac? Small?'

The women shrugged and we laughed. It didn't matter. They were just thrilled to have seen the animals bounding across their path, a rare sight in this human-filled forest.

Close to the entrance again, the wood was busy with people. Children were building a den with their mother. A father and toddler were pulling a sledge. The father proudly showed me his handiwork, the decorative curves of the side panels made with his jigsaw cutter, neat joins between the body of the sledge and the wooden runners.

'I'm just waiting for the metal gliders I ordered to arrive,' he said as his son danced around us, poking us with his finger. 'They should be here tomorrow.'

I waved goodbye to the father and toddler and carried on. What was it about snow that encouraged us to lose our inhibitions and chat to strangers? Perhaps it was just the joy of the transformed landscape and the radiance of sky, ground and tree. Perhaps, it was the oddness of a woman skiing in this small British forest that made walkers stop and enquire with curiosity. I didn't know. I was just glad after the weeks of lockdown to have face-to-face encounters – rich in the fellowship of humans and intoxication of snow.

The Thaw

If winter comes can spring be far behind?
– Percy Bysshe Shelley

For the rest of the week, the temperature stayed below freezing. Mornings were bright and filled with blue. But the heat of the sun threatened the snow covering, and there were no fresh falls. The new week would bring rain and temperatures soaring to 10 degrees. I had two or three days left to ski. I circled Darwin Forest, broke into its holiday complex and skied across virgin snow.

But the thaw was coming too fast. I drove to Cuckoostone Lane where Tom and I had listened to the eponymous bird one spring, at first a distant smudge in the air, then a sharp fluted two-note growing louder as we drew closer. I wondered when the lane had been named and how long the cuckoo had made this place its home. Centuries, perhaps. I planned to ski to the end of the lane then return through the forest, but when I arrived the sun had already melted the snow. I drove on to the top of the plantation on East Moor. A few hundred feet higher and the world was still white. A broad path dropped through the woodland, icy with small stones poking through. I set off cautiously, not liking the steepness of the path, not liking the stones. As soon as I could, I took a smaller path to the left. The way was flatter and there were fewer stones, but soon I came to a large trunk that blocked the path. I turned right to drop down again through the forest clearing. This too was difficult as the snow had sunk under the footprints in the marshy ground. Beaten, I took off my skis and walked to the path at the bottom. Here, the forest track had a good covering and I could ski unhindered. It swept round to the main path I had left behind. I turned again and followed the path to the edge of the plantation. I stopped and took in the view of the plateau – white on black – forest and snowfield. The sky was an electric blue, the edges of the fields shadow grey. Winter days like these, I could happily inhabit. I turned around and placed my skis in the tracks I'd made and followed the incline back to the main path.

Below me was a newer plantation of young pines. Tom and I had gone there one evening at the beginning of summer just as the light was fading out. A song thrush had sung sweetly from somewhere within the forest, but we had been on the hunt for another bird. We edged the nursery, listening carefully. Then we heard it! Quiet, at first, then louder as we drew closer. At first, there was a high whirling noise, then a lower, slower sound as if its battery was running out. Then a *clack, clack, clack*. A nightjar! What a privilege it had been to hear this comical bird call. What a privilege it had been to watch the darkness fall on that warm evening on the edge of summer. We sat on a log, enjoying the stillness of the forest, thrilled to hear this endangered bird.

Here in my winter present, the woodland was silent, but the landscape sang its radiant beauty. The sun was strong now, the snow pocked, grasses poking through. By the entrance to the wood, I took off my skis and tried to push them upright into the snow, only succeeding after several attempts. The melt was coming fast. Soon, the plateau above Matlock would be green again. I held my face to the sun, enjoying its feeble warmth, enjoying the electricity of the winter brightness. Before long, it would be gone. Back home, I wrote in my gratitude diary: *Light, light, light! The purity of air. The snow-covered forest.*

Transitioning

The fairest thing in nature, a flower still has its
roots in earth and manure.
– D.H. Lawrence

The earth was stirring. Snowdrops crowded banks, delicate pearly white flowers against the vivid green of fresh leaf. Catkins hung from hazel bushes, dripping pale lemon from leafless branches. Above Cromford, the familiarity of the landscape was comforting, Masson Hill, High Tor and Matlock strung out across the Bank below Farley and Bottom forests. This was home.

I came to a three-way junction, where Intake Lane meets the High Peak Trail. I left the dismantled railway to follow the lane that was just an earthen track through forest. The sun shone on the mossy skirts of beeches, luminous, the edges of birch trunks chalked in white. Rooks called from treetops and a coal tit tried out his voice. Intake Lane, now flanked by dry stone walls, turned away from the woodland to drop down through fields. I was learning to enjoy my solitary walks in winter's nature. I paid more attention to its detail – how the contours of the land connected woodland with woodland, dale with dale, escarpment with moor, moorland with sky. I climbed a field and joined a farm track, a bank of pale crocuses outside a stone cottage unfolding hearts of yolk. The world was filled with delicate beauty and a promise of renewed colour. The air had a touch of warmth. I felt a lightness of foot that comes when the earth emerges from its winter sleep.

A few days later, Tom and I plotted a ramble around the village of Elton. We crossed Elton Common, a desert of green that rose and fell to a distant horizon. But in this featureless landscape, there was life. The burble of skylark rose from newly seeded grass. It was a sound I'd not heard since visiting Rimac Nature Reserve on the saltmarshes of the Lincolnshire coast. First, we saw a pair, then a trio low in the field before dropping into the vegetation. Their song was still subdued, far from reaching the dizzying exuberance of spring and summer. Over the next rise and fall, there was more and more lark song on the air, the music sweet and thrilling, a promise of longer days and summer heat. On the edge of Long Dale, one lark hovered higher over the grasslands, its song more vivacious. I knew that the acrobatic flight displays and tumbling songs that would rise and fall with the fullness of spring were far from reaching their crescendo. This was still the prelude.

As we dropped down into Deep Dale – a deep slash across the belly of the Peak – two buzzards wheeled in the sky above us. Effortlessly, they surfed a thermal. Their ease of movement in the blue sky puffed with cloud spoke to my earthbound human soul. My spirit soared with the birds. As we walked into the hollowed out dale, grassy runway gave way to gravel and shrubby hillside. Underground streams bubbled to the surface and found their way down our path. I splashed through clear water, the pebbles of limestone, smooth and rounded beneath my feet, making a satisfying crunch. Water gave way to meadow. On the rocky tor of Mock Beggar Hall, we spread ourselves out on a flat bed of rock, feeling a trickle of sun on our faces. Spring was fickle in its warmth, I knew that, but the birdsong that was growing with each passing day and the unfurling of the first flowers told me there was no going back.

Waterside

L'acqua è la forza motrice di tutta la natura.
(Water is the driving force of all nature.)
– Leonardo da Vinci

Winter lay in the valley, spring on the uplands. In Ashford-in-the-Water, snowdrops trailed across the grassy bank next to a sheep pen. Here, the sheep are washed clean as they are driven across the water, then sheared in a centuries-old tradition. As I followed the Wye, the soft sound of water in my ears, I felt a cleansing too. Tom and I padded along the winding riverside path to a stone mill, two waterwheels at the end of the gables. Soon, we were climbing through woods. The leaves and shoots of wildflowers were beginning to push through the ground. Bluebells, I imagined. And wild garlic. We turned left to climb the wall of the valley, so steep I had to use the wire mesh that ran alongside the dry stone wall to pull myself up. Then, we were on top, out of the shadows and into the sunshine. We reached Sheldon and careered down meadows towards the Wye again. The Peak opened out to reveal Ashford, its hall and parkland, the inky patches of forest and the bump of moorland beyond. And with the light and space and heat of sun, there was an opening up of my heart.

'Wait,' I said to Tom. 'I want to sunbathe.'

We lay down on the grass, backs against a dry stone wall. I held my face to the heat and absorbed the stillness of the Peak, feeling its warmth flow through my body, slowing my breathing, quietening my mind. There was just the hum of air and bird and water. Its music sang to me, soft and hopeful. We were in this place that straddled winter and spring, the dark and the light, the cold and the warmth. I had been here before – every year of my life – and every year it felt like the first time.

* * *

The Wye Valley is a place of healing, its waters, meadows and woodlands. Tom and I returned on that last spring-warm trio of days to follow the river north and west. Winter and spring blended. The light was soft and warm. In the shadows, the river meadow was ice green, the woodlands above golden brown in the sunlight. A weir ahead thundered over the drop. In summer, we had seen dippers here, tails bobbing as they ducked for weeds and minnows, the water dappled marine blue and aqua green. Ahead, the Monsal Head Viaduct cuts across the loop of river, its weathered stone and its great arches suitably majestic with the sweep of the sheer-sided Wye. Now the railway was silent, the dismantled line edged with herbs and wildflowers in spring and summer, the tunnels dripping water, the blasted rock covered in moss and lichen. The viaduct, mirrored upside down in the Wye, seemed to belong to the hills and the water. Downstream, the river steamed. Moorhens and mallards took shelter in the reeds. We climbed the ash woods onto a stony track and found another open meadow on top of the dale that echoed the one beside the river below. Sheep drank from a dew pond, cloud and wool reflected in the water. Across the valley, a long sweep of ridge cut a line above the woods, dark and brooding, but beyond that the contours of moorland edges stretched out in shades of palest blue. Below, the Wye Valley wound through the Peak. Somewhere behind us, the faint song of the skylark called to us across the uplands. We ate our sandwiches, then lay down and absorbed the heat of the sun and the sounds of the sky. This spring warmth was temporary, I knew that. March had a way of torturing; there would be winter gales one day, mild sunshine the next. But I was grateful for this glimpse into the future. Winter would cling on but soon it would yield for good – until the next one.

The Second Winter

Widening Horizons

November

Coastal Highs

I must go down to the sea today, to the lonely sea and the sky.
– John Masefield

Winter followed by spring is as immutable as birth and death. When the season of light and growth slipped in, something inside me unfurled. Despite my tentative affair with winter, spring seduced me like an old lover and the grey was forgotten. Our evening walks through darkness into light hit me with an intensity I'd never felt before. The light! The colour! Renewed life pushed through the warming earth: the first pale snowdrops; crocuses and dwarf hyacinths filling the air with scent; primroses delicate on the banks of country lanes; wood anemone brightening dark woods; pungent garlic. And the buttercups spilling gold on Masson Hill as we climbed it. The light lingering into evening was sweet. I was intoxicated. There was no question: my sense of well-being improved in spring. My mood lifted. I felt lighter, more energetic. Winter, I admitted to myself, didn't penetrate my mind and soul like spring and summer did.

As another winter approached, I reflected on the previous one. Had anything changed? What had I learned? What had helped? What had hindered? Sometimes, I felt I suffered nothing more than the winter blues and mild anxiety, not the crippling depression some people experienced with full-blown Seasonal Affective Disorder. Other times, it felt debilitating. Looking back, I saw there had been lots of factors that had made the previous winter easier. Keeping a winter journal had made a significant difference: the act of writing my observations down helped change my mind-set. I had observed the winter landscape more carefully. I learned to appreciate its subtler beauty and my relationship with it had become more positive. My conscious effort to rewrite the narrative of winter, physically and mentally, had worked, at least on the days I was open to it. In writing my feelings down, it felt like I was giving myself therapy sessions.

Spending more time outside had especially helped. I was more in tune with the way winter is part of the circular nature of life – as our ancient ancestors had observed and celebrated. Prehistoric humans, having no electricity, oil or candlelight, lived within the perimeters of the seasons and a day's length. They ate well in times of plenty, stored up food for lean times, and conserved their energy for lighter days when they could hunt and gather for longer. I'd seen how nature slowed down to conserve energy until spring. I was still not entirely in sync with winter; I still had to adhere to the rhythm to the season with conviction as nature did. It was a lesson I was still learning.

Being outside also provided me with light that lifted my mood. When I could, I'd headed into the countryside on bright, sunny days. Scientists are not convinced that SAD is caused by lack of light, but I knew from experience sunlit days immediately lightened me. Our walks in the dark had been a surprise, however. I loved the way a new world opened up under the mantle of darkness. With the sense of sight reduced, my sense of smell and hearing had taken precedent. It drew me more intimately into the moment.

There were three kinds of winter landscapes (apart from the snowscapes I loved so much) that had especially helped: forests, wide-open spaces and sea. For the coming winter, I resolved to seek them out more. There were days, of course, when I'd failed to convince myself of a different narrative. These were short days when the sky was a lid of grey and the rain relentless. I still had some way to go to embrace the British winter fully, but I reminded myself of the words of American writer Thomas Wentworth Higginson: *How many lessons of faith and beauty we should lose, if there were no winter in our year?*

And so, summer slipped into autumn and back into winter, the changes so gradual I barely noticed then. That September, I spent days chopping and stewing apples from our little apple tree, almost doubled over with the weight of its outsized apples. Tom gathered damsons and made jam, then gin. Windows steamed. I lit the wood burner. The cherry tree shed its leaves, leaving a carpet coloured by Indian golden spice. Skeletal trees reached for darkening skies. Covid had still not left us, changing shape and always one step ahead of the scientists, but it least the havoc it had previously wreaked was lessening. Precautionary measures were still in place but there were no more lockdowns. We were learning to live with the virus.

As autumn eased out, I yearned for winter seas again. The previous December in lockdown, I'd written to the Lincolnshire police to ask if I could visit the seals at Donna Nook. I wanted to write about them. 'No,' came the reply, and there was nothing more I could do. The sea was out of bounds, and I had to learn to live within the borders of my landlocked Derbyshire. This time, I could go.

We returned to Wales, my doctor husband and I, picking up our elder would-be-doctor son in Swansea before continuing to Pembrokeshire. Our rented cabin lay stuffed into the side of a coastal valley. We could just step out and the sea was ours. We tumbled down a narrow path through shrub and woodland to a deep cove caught in the hug of two headlands. Dune and grasses gave way to pebble and sand, the sea a sheet of glass at Norton Haven. Above us, the sky was powdered blue, the winter bathing everything in glistening light. Sometimes the path was steep as a mountain track, my lungs clawing at the salty air. Sea cliffs and stacks plunged to the ocean below. Descending to inlets, we crunched through pebbles that almost appeared translucent in the wash of hillside run-off and winter light. Peaty streams poured off the hilltops down to the sea, the gorse yellow-bright. The air was cool but the sun strong. How different it was from that rainy weekend in Carmarthenshire the year before. Here at Newgale, the water-lacquered beach was tinged sky blue, spume misting the coast. On the shore, breakers frothed white, surfers catching the waves. Dogs flounced out to sea and padded over sands. A solitary figure sat on his surfboard and stared out at the surging Irish Sea. I felt alive in a way only the ocean could make me feel. *If only I could live by the sea.*

Later in the day, sunlight split the gathering charcoal clouds, casting pools of radiant light on the water. It was all that I could wish for – the thrust and chill of winter softened by the glow of summer-warm sun.

Storm Watching

Blow, blow thou winter wind.
– William Shakespeare

We had been gifted a return to summer in Pembrokeshire. In Swedish, it's called *grävlingssommar* – badger summer – when the long-snouted animals have a second unexpected chance to sniff out more winter supplies. Latvians call it *atvasara*, the Dutch *nazomer*, meaning late or second summer. From my days living in Germany, I knew the word *Altweibersommer* – old woman's summer. The Swiss call it *Witwesömmerli* – the widower's little summer. I liked the Spanish 'Quince Summer', where lingering November sunny days ripen the fruit, ready for picking. The Anglo-Saxons called it St Martin's Summer, St Martin's Day taking place in the middle of November. Whatever name you give to the return of summer in the early throes of winter, it's fleeting, disappearing as quickly as it arrives and more precious for its unexpected return.

On the Pembrokeshire coast, warmth and sunlight quickly yielded to cold and grey. By midweek, the skies had darkened again, and the rain began to fall. Wind followed. Marloes Peninsula was not the best choice for coastal walking with gales blowing off the sea. Here, we found one of Pembrokeshire's most ragged and inhospitable coastlines at St Brides Bay. The peninsula juts out into the treacherous Jack Sound, a graveyard of shipwrecks, with an exposed Skomer island beyond. It felt like a forgotten place – at least in a winter storm.

Country lanes rise and dip to Marloes Mere. The wetlands and ponds lying at the eastern end of the peninsula are home to garganey, teal and sedge warblers. The once desert fields, stripped of wildlife, have been returned to heathland, the call of meadow pipit and stonechat a familiar sound rising out of the heather. We dropped down a gravel path, passing a white-washed cottage. The clouds hung low, a band of pale light on the horizon. Marloes Sands came into view, small, pointed rocks thrusting out of the rocky shoreline like sharks' teeth: the Raggle Rocks. Beyond the beach, the flat-topped Gatesholm Island lay squat on the water like a sleeping dog. We sat on the shingle, hunched up against the wind, eating our picnic lunch. Layers of grey shale and red sandstone rose near vertically out of the rock-strewn beach. The whole coast is layered with volcanic rock and sandstones as if some giant had scored the cliffs with a fork. The surf thrashed against the rocks. This is a wild place – a place to come in winter when the tide thrusts itself against the sea-blasted shore and throws up spray. We picked our way through rock pools and a debris of stones, running back from the incoming tide, feeling the sea's foam on our faces and its salt on our lips. It was thrilling. The force of the sea shook me awake out of my winter stupor. I felt its energy. I felt its power. The onshore winds slammed my body, shoved fistfuls of salty air down my throat. Waves crashed violently against the Raggle Rocks. There was no other place I wanted to be.

I started up the cliff onto the top, Tom and Jamie following reluctantly behind; neither of them liked drops, even less so in wind. The path narrowed to nothing more than a sheep track. The cliffs fell vertically to Albion Sands where the eponymous paddle steamer ran aground with its cargo of pigs and whisky in 1837. Here it was again: the heightened feeling of danger that shook me awake, the feeling of being metaphorically and physically on the edge, the sea offering up its energy, offering up its light. I felt my heart quicken, my sluggish edge-of-winter brain coming to. The wind slammed my body. I loved the thrill of the danger. This was it was to live – shaken, slammed by the wind, thrown about.

Tom felt differently. He refused to go further, leaning into the path's bank as if the wind would snatch him away. There was no arguing. We took another path further back from the cliff edge. I caught glimpses of the tattered coastline, the waves blasting caves, stacks, rock piles, cliff faces and stony inlets. Their names reflect this place of winter: Rainy Rock; Pitting Gales Point; Deadman's Bay. This was a coastline not to mess with.

The Seals

To unpathed waters, undreamed shores.
– William Shakespeare

In the car park above Martin's Haven, the rain came on. We hesitated, not sure if the steep drop down to the harbour was worth a soaking. As we stood there pondering, a woman told us there were Atlantic grey seals below the slipway.

I had forgotten the seals of Donna Nook, but now here in Wales I had another chance. The rain came down harder as we climbed down the steps to the slipway. In the distance, at the other end of the deep shingle beach, I could see one cow and two pups on the pebbles, a second cow drifting on the surf. I saw steps leading along the side of the hillside above the cove would give me good views of the Atlantic greys. From a respectful distance, I had a good view of the sea mammals resting on dry land. One of the pups was already plump and well rounded, its fur snow white. It must have been one or two weeks old. The other pup, lying off to one side, looked smaller than the white and had already moulted its downy fur. It was leaner, probably a week or two older, and its skin had taken on a smooth grey sheen. The blubbery cow, having spotted me on the cliffside above, eyed me warily but didn't shift from its place at the bottom of the cliff. Just offshore, her companion drifted in the water, sometimes disappearing below the surface of the sea to reappear some yards away. Once it turned over on its back, its broad nose to the air, flippers tucked to its chest, rounded face, rounded eyes. Child sweet. It called to the other cow, its bark ringing round the harbour, and the other female clumsily belly-flopped towards the water in response, then thinking better of it, belly-flopped back to her pup. On land, seals look ugly, their blubber wobbling as they clumsily drag their deadweight along the shingle. In water, they become sleek and elegant, smooth skin taking on an oily lacquered look, bodies lithe as they slice through the water. We watched the seals for about a quarter of an hour, those fifteen minutes condensed to the Atlantic greys, and the drizzle.

Beyond the pathway I stood on, a metal gangway dropped down to the water where summer boats depart for Skomer. A Marine Conservation Area, the island is home to a riot of razorbills, guillemots, puffins, fulmars, shags, cormorants, Manx shearwater and storm petrels. In winter, the puffins head out into the North Atlantic somewhere – where exactly, nobody knows. Kittiwakes, like the puffins, head for the deeper waters of the Atlantic, while guillemots and razorbills prefer the safety of the Continental shelf. Fulmars, shags and cormorants stick close to their nesting grounds. Storm petrels head for Africa and Manx shearwaters for Argentina: they are not hanging around for winter.

I left Pembrokeshire for home, grateful for the badger summer, grateful for the energy of the ocean in the swell of early winter, grateful for the winds and rains. Grateful for the wild seas and the Atlantic greys. All of it breathed life into my shored-up winter body.

December

A Walk in the Polar Twilight

In order for the light to shine so brightly,
the darkness must be present.
– Sir Francis Bacon

I envied the storm petrels and shearwaters of Skomer their freedom to migrate unhindered by borders or Covid. I too wanted to migrate like the birds. I loved my island but my *fernweh*, my 'away-sickness', after a period of lockdown contentment had returned with fervour. I wanted to revisit the extreme cold and darkness of the Arctic I'd experienced in Kittilä and dive again into the polar night. I wanted to find out more precisely why the Lappish Finns seemed unaffected by the darkness.

It seems an odd wish – to swap the shortened hours of daylight on my damp Atlantic island for the perpetual dusk and darkness of the frozen Lapland south of the Barents Sea. But when I'd visited the Arctic Circle that first time in winter, I'd fallen in love with its dreamlike snowscapes and delicate colours brushing the twilight. I wrote to Visit Finland and received an invitation to join a group of travel journalists. I realised I was in a privileged position having access to funded travel as a freelance travel writer: it was giving me the opportunity to explore attitudes to winter in other countries.

* * *

At 60 degrees north, the lakes and forests surrounding Helsinki were already frozen, the sky succumbing to blackness mid-afternoon. It wasn't enough. I travelled north another 500 miles to Rovaniemi, a place edging the Arctic Circle. Night had already fallen when I reached my hotel on the confluence of the Ounasjoki and the Kemijoki rivers. Outside my window candle-shaped lights shone on top of the white poles of Jätkänkynttilä (the Lumberjack's Candle Bridge), reflecting in the free-flowing currents of the rivers' meeting place. On the waterside, streetlights bathed the road in a sheen of electric white, the verges puckered icing and the branches and barks of birches blasted white. Even the wooden fence was snow-sprayed.

Why did I love the Arctic so much?

The pale night, the silence of snow, winter stillness.

I had a day alone in Rovaniemi the administrative capital of Finland's Lapland, a bustling city – more town-sized – set down in the silence of snowbound forest and hill. In World War II, Rovaniemi was almost obliterated by German forces, who had ruthlessly employed scorched earth tactics. Few pre-War buildings survive. Now it's primarily a city of apartment blocks with balconies glass-proofed against the harsh Arctic winter and summer mosquitoes. Between the warren-like shopping malls, brightly lit Christmas trees softened the angular lines of the city centre, but it was the curve of water and hill beyond the city's harsh geometry I wanted to explore.

Outside, the -20°C temperature caught my throat and numbed my toes and fingertips. I had a choice: turn left to walk along the banks of the Ounasjoki or right along Kemijoki River. I turned left. It didn't take long to leave the city behind. In front of me, mist smoked off the frozen river. Boats, benches and lifebuoys lay under layers of snow, reminding me summer – of sorts – existed in Rovaniemi, white yielding to forest green. Now, it seemed unimaginable. Everything was uncanny here. Sounds were muffled except for the creak and crunch of snow underfoot, the air glass in my throat, scraping my lungs and anaesthetising my body. My tongue felt thick, the muscle sluggish. Dog walkers marched briskly through the woods, heads bent against the flurries of snow, eyelashes frosted white, hair silvered at their tips. I called '*Hei*' to passers, but no one responded. Was it the city mentality? Or had I rudely interrupted the Finns' love of silence? I didn't know.

It felt strange to be trudging alone through the snow in this unfamiliar landscape, where locals passed without as much as a nod. I felt like a ghost. Soon, I left the city's dog walkers behind. There was just me, the trees, the frozen river and the snow. The absolute silence and stillness when I stopped made me feel exposed. There were no distractions. Once again, I was stripped bare. Slowly, I tuned into the riverside landscape. The snow was invigorating, its brightness a hit, even in the subdued light of the far north. I let go of my anxiety, stepped out of my head and into the otherworldliness of the Arctic. This! This was why I had come back to Lapland.

The path weaved between silver birches and firs. I settled into the stillness. I came to a wooden shelter, a bit like a tepee, but solid and with one side open to the elements. The Finns call it a *lavvu*, or lean-to, and they use them for barbecues. *Lavvu* comes from the Sami language, from a time when the indigenous people built portable shelters with forked branches and covered them in reindeer hides. There were fresh ashes on the fire pit, I noted. Finns will happily trek to a *lavvu* in sub-zero temperatures to grill sausages in the snow. Tree stumps and logs surrounding the firepit provided seating, a large shed with a sliding door stacked with free logs. Eventually, I came to the end of the forest path. The river was wider here and solidly frozen. I could see the tracks of snowmobiles and someone walking on the river. I dared to take a few steps onto the Ounasjoki. Beyond this point, the river flows in and through river islands: Madesaari, Koivusaari, Suutarinsaari, Selkäsaari, lietesaari. The Finnish language is a minefield of vowels, impossible to remember or spell. The trick, I realised, was to break it down: *saari* means island; *joki*, river. My knowledge of Finnish, admittedly, was still purely geographical: *joki, saari, lumi* – snow!

The Finns have at least forty words for snow and the conditions associated with them. Many of these words can be translated directly into English: snowstorm, hail, sleet, ice and frost. But there are many more we don't have in English and require a whole sentence to describe. Later in the day, when I walked in the opposite direction along Kemijoki from Rovaniemi, I saw *röpelö* – uneven ice, a frozen echo of waves on the water. Further on, the river was a mess of churned-up ice, as if some ogre had taken an axe to it: *ahtauma*.

The word for snow, however, in this Uralic language, appears to have its roots in Latin: *lumineux* in Old French; *luminosus* in Latin; luminous in English – from the Latin root *lumen,* light; figuratively the light of life. The day was overcast, the sky dulled in dusk, yet everything was luminous – the frozen river, the trees and hills. There was so much joy in this Arctic fringe. A cleansing. The light of life in the polar twilight.

Creatures of the Arctic

Eteenpäin sanoi mummo lumessa.
(Forward, said the granny in the snow.)
– Finnish proverb

Timo speaks with a voice full of gravel. He's bent over a raging pit fire, a frozen Arctic landscape behind him.

'My grandfather always told me Päivätär would come back one day – the Goddess of the Sun.' In Finnish mythology, Päivätär owns the silver of the sun, spins it into yarn then weaves it into clothes and jewellery.

This is how the Salla video begins. The next shot shows a white-out Salla. Unlike Rovaniemi, hovering on the Arctic Circle line, Salla – where I now found myself – lay well clear of it. The video returns to Timo. He's skiing at speed across a snowbound meadow, pulled by a reindeer and dressed only in shorts and ski boots and waving a large Olympian flag.

'Here we will build a huge stadium,' he shouts as his skis lift into the air.

'Warm heart – we have it.'

'Warm place, coming soon,' a woman chips in.

Other inhabitants demonstrate 'beach' volleyball – 'the snow will turn to sand' – Olympic swimming, athletics, surfing and mountain biking. On the surface, the video appears to be presenting Salla's bid for the Summer Olympics 2032, but it's a spoof. Its real purpose is to raise awareness of climate breakdown.

I had travelled from Rovaniemi to Salla by minibus, two hours north-east towards the Russian border, this time with a different set of journalists and Heidi, our Salla guide. Arriving at Salla Wilderness Park, I didn't recognise Timo from the video I'd watched back home.

Our guide for the morning, he greeted us with a look of good-humoured mischief. He wore a Russian *ushanka*, a fur hat with ear flaps, and a thin cagoule made from deer hide, his thick red beard giving him extra warmth. We followed him out of the visitor centre to harnessed reindeer clipped to sleighs. With a drollness typical of the Finns, Timo gave us instructions on how to drive the reindeer.

'The reindeer don't like to be patted,' he said solemnly. 'It reminds them of the mosquitoes in summer.' He ran a finger along the reindeer's back and it gave a shimmy.

'In the carriage, you can lie back like you're on the beach. Relax, you're on holiday!' He stretched out on the reindeer hides to demonstrate. 'But best not put your feet out.' He demonstrated again. 'It would be a shame to lose them.'

I was assigned Antti, the elder reindeer, feasting on snow at the back of the convoy. As he was the most experienced deer, I assumed this was why he was bringing up the rear. But Antti had a mind of his own. Soon, we were dragging behind. Timo's assistant Paula came to the rescue, hopping on the runner footboard at the back of the sleigh.

'*Mene, mene, mene,*' Paula coaxed, but Antti was not to be hurried as the other reindeer sleighs disappeared over the dip.

'*Ss, ss, ss.*' Go, go, go.

There would be a spurt of movement then Antti would stop to muzzle the snow again.

'*Mene, mene, men*e,' I echoed Paula. '*Ss, ss, ss.*'

Antti turned his head and gave me a withering look as if to say my Finnish left a lot to be desired, then stopped to graze more snow at the side of the track. I stopped worrying and chatted to Paula, noticing the sheaved knife strapped to her waist. Timo, I'd spotted, had three.

'I never go shopping for meat,' Paula told me. 'Everything in my freezer, I've shot myself or with the hunting club.'

Finland has a long hunter-gatherer history unbroken over thousands of years. Autumn is a time of gathering in Lapland. Preserved lingonberries, bilberries, cloudberries, cranberries, raspberries and Arctic brambles add sunshine to food in winter. Wild herbs and mushrooms gathered from the forest floor in autumn also flavour meat. In the polar night, I ate reindeer fillet with wild thyme sauce and white fish caught in the nearby lakes served with morel sauce. I tried Lappish cheese with Arctic cloudberries – the food of Päivätär the Sun Goddess. Locally caught fish is part of many meals: salmon, white fish, vendace, char, trout, pike and perch. Reindeer is served every way imaginable, from burgers and pizza to soup, its blood pancake a speciality.

The reindeer, though semi-wild, are farmed, sometimes tracked across scores of miles through the taiga. Generally, there's no moral dilemma about eating meat in Lapland where only the hardiest of vegetables grow in the short summer season. Laplanders know where their food came from, and nothing is wasted. The carbon footprint of the hunter is that of human tracks in a nearby forest.

Timo also loved fishing, I learned. He called himself a 'selective fisherman', releasing the 'ones important to the river' and keeping the small adult males – regulation permitting. Timo and Paula both hunted for game, mostly capercaillie and black grouse. It struck me hunting isn't an emotive subject in the Arctic Circle, nor is it associated with the upper classes. Hunting is 'everyman's right', albeit tightly regulated by limited licences, and it's a community activity. In Lapland, I observed a respect for, and a love of, nature alongside a hunting culture that would seem like a contradiction to many Brits. For Finns, there is none.

We came to a stop in the middle of the forest, great flames rising out of the firepit.

'Now we do yoga,' Timo announced, a glint in his eye.

'First, we spread the hands over the fire like this.' Timo spread his hands out in a smooth yoga-like move. 'Palms down.' The heat felt good after the chill of the polar twilight.

'Now, the backs of the hands.' He turned his hands with a flourish. 'And now for the most difficult move.' He hesitated, then turned his back to the fire, arms extended in a flow, and leaned his bottom into the heat.

As we headed out on the sleighs again, the sun leaked gold on the horizon and flamed firs. In front of us, the tops of the snowbound trees were tipped in ice-cream pink. I thought about the toughness of these Lappish Finns and their affinity with nature. They were a people who preferred to be outdoors whatever the temperature. They embraced winter. They embraced the polar night. They embraced their part in nature's eco-chain. At home, there was no polar night or frozen landscapes. It was a very different winter experience. Instead, we had the big skies of wide-open spaces, the reflected light of sea and shallows, the shafts of lights reaching down in small forests. I needed to embrace my very British version of winter. I needed to develop an even closer relationship with the outdoors and nature. This was what Timo and Paula were teaching me.

The next morning as we walked up Iso-Pyhättunturi Sallatunturi (*tunturi* the Finnish word for a Lapland fell), I thought about the deer.

As we'd fed the young moss in the corral, Paula had pointed to a handsome pure white youth. 'The baby white calves are vulnerable. They are easily seen in the early summer after they're born. It's easy for an eagle to spot their pale coats in the darker green and pick them off.'

But there is a more serious threat to the entire reindeer population. Reindeer have evolved to thrive in the Arctic conditions. In winter, their soft footpads shrink, leaving exposed sharp hoof rims that enable them to dig deep into the snow to reach moss and lichen. As temperatures rise and fluctuate in the Arctic Circle, rain freezes on snow leaving a thick layer of ice – *kaljama* – and the reindeer are unable to access their food. In a world where humans and reindeer are interdependent, climate change is a real threat.

But as we climbed the fell, I forgot the reindeer and I tuned into the moment: the candle spruces bent over with the weight of snow, great chunks of snow frozen in the trees – *tykky* – their branches weirdly fattened and misshapen. Rabbit and bird tracks crisscrossed the hillside, but otherwise there was no sign of wildlife. Inge-Maaret, our guide from Parks and Wildlife Finland, told us the wildlife was all around us, just buried under a layer of snow for warmth. I remembered Timo telling us the previous day that the large black capercaillies also bury themselves in the snow, leaving airholes so they can still breathe, and how, if disturbed, they shoot out of the snow, raising a cloud of white, wings flapping wildly. Flushing out game took on a whole new meaning in the Arctic Circle.

We felt our way over boardwalks covered in snow, trying not to lose our balance so as not to fall into the snow-covered bog. Silence. A world devoid of life. Or not. We turned a corner and saw a solitary willow grouse circling a birch. We stood and watched the grouse for several minutes, its pure white feathers tipped black. It was a moment of serene beauty.

I asked Inge-Maaret about the Finnish love of silence.

'Yes, it's true. We don't much like small talk. We're comfortable with silence when we're with others. I think it's because we spend so much time in nature. We're used to the quiet of the wilderness. We welcome it.'

I thought about this. The Finnish reserve could easily be read as melancholy, but I wondered if the opposite was true, at least in the Arctic. The Finns I met in Lapland seemed to be in tune with their environment, focused on being present. There were no chattering voices inside or outside their heads, I imagined. I too felt the stillness and ease of being in the Arctic Circle.

Ahead, we lost the trodden path and sunk into deep snow. Tall conifers gave way to dwarfed vegetation then a boulder field. Mist obscured our views, the forests and lakes in the valley below hidden from sight. Arriving at a wooden staircase, we clutched the rail as we ascended the ice-covered steps. Then, through the mist, a frosted observation post came into view, a Doctor Zhivago-esque ice palace. We climbed more ice-covered steps to the viewpoint.

'Out there,' Heidi said, pointing into the mists, 'is Russia.'

Somewhere in those mists was old Salla, a village that had once belonged to Finland. Timo's grandfather had come from there, he'd told us as we'd warmed our hands over the firepit. During the Winter War, the Russians had invaded Finland at

Salla. The Finns had pushed them back, then ceded old Salla with a handful of other settlements after the war. In the Continuation War of World War II, the Germans had occupied those areas with the support of the Finns; afterwards, old Salla was ceded for a second time. The Finns who found themselves on the wrong side of the border were resettled.

We gazed out at the endless Russian taiga into old Finland.

'We could just walk over the border,' I joked.

'Not a good idea,' Heidi said dryly. 'Two international students thought it would be fun to sneak through the forest and over the boundary, but there are trackers everywhere. They were caught and won't be welcomed back in Finland or Russia any day soon.'

I envied the animals who wandered back and forth across the border at will. Suddenly, I had an urge to travel deeper into the frozen wastes of Russia, through endless forests and on into the Urals of Siberia, where the wilderness was even harsher and more expansive. How did the Siberians cope with the some of the world's most severe winter weather conditions? A seed had been planted.

Black is the Night, Bright is the Land

De nacht is levendiger en rijker gekleurd dan de dag. (The night is more alive and more richly coloured than the day.)
– Vincent van Gogh

As far as I know, Vincent van Gogh never travelled to the Nordic countries, yet his night paintings capture the electricity of the Arctic. The swirling movements of Van Gogh echo the dance of the aurora borealis. In Kittilä, the skies had been clearer, the green sheen of the northern lights a glow in the sky, the Milky Way, a path of stardust; meteor showers like fireworks. Stars flickering. In the Lappish twilight, the sky glowed violet and bluish pink, colouring fells and tops of firs in pastel shades. In Salla, low-lying cloud hid the theatre of lights, but even in the mists the night sky appeared a soft cobalt blue.

When darkness leans into the pale Arctic landscape, the snow seems bizarrely brighter, whiter – full of light.

Down in the valley where we met Vladimir, our fat-bike guide, under the polar night, the wind whipped up snow, a chilly blast cutting through every layer of clothing. As we cycled up into the forest, stillness descended, the mist-smudged sky wrapping forest and fell in wool. We focused on our breathing as we pedalled up a lane surrounded by firs and birches, and concentrated on keeping the fat-bikes in the grooves tyres had made on the forest track. The tyres of the fat-bikes were comically thick with a deep tread, but still it was difficult to keep the handlebars straight. A slip left or right meant the wheel caught the bank of snow – followed by a powdery landing.

Ahead, my cycling companions spread out along the track, seeking solitude. The silence spoke to us. The Arctic sky cradled us. The snow bathed us. The track began to climb, the beams of our bikes casting a long light between the conifers. Eventually, the ground began to flatten out; we had reached the top of the fell. Vladimir picked up a handful of snow and let it sift through his fingers. It fell like dust – *viti*.

'It's powder dry. There's no precipitation in the air here so the snow doesn't compact. That's why we make artificial snow for the ski slope.'

Across the valley, the floodlit ski *piste* spilled off the adjacent fell in a river of light. But here in the shadows, the night covered us, and the snow had a soft glow that held me. Heading back down the hill, it was even more difficult to keep the handlebars straight. I fell again and again, snow puffing into the air. I rolled over like a puppy, my giggles filling the night air as I struggled to my knees then back onto my bike. It was both exhausting and thrilling. At last, we reached the compacted forest road again. I flew down into the valley, the rush of cold air in my face. It was exhilarating, all of it – the speed, the swallowing darkness, the pale luminous snow. I was in love with the dark. I was in love with the light.

On our last day, we were invited to explore a nearby fell called Ruuhitunturi by snowmobile. I had mixed feelings about the machines: they broke the silence of the woodland and filled the pure Arctic air with the fumes of fuel. At the same time, I loved the thrill of the ride, the speed on the snow, the lurch of heart and machine on the curves.

The snowmobiles roared across the low-lying fell, rising and falling with the contours of the forest. The trees were ghosts and the track a spill of shining gloss from the machines' beams, the forest beyond filled with shadows. We'd entered a dark fable. We climbed to a high spot with another ice-encrusted observation point, then dropped down to the *kahvila*, a remote wilderness café. The wood-encased cabin was dark, candle lamps giving out faint glows of light on each bench. The walls above the bar were hung with antlers and the fanned feathers of capercaillies – Salla's emblem. The only other light came from the flames of a wood burner. We drank coffee and ate cinnamon buns, our hands cupping the hot drinks for warmth. In the dimness of the nest-like room, we spoke in hushed voices. Outside, the forest was the smallest whisper. For three days, the Arctic had held me in its iced breath. Tomorrow, I was going home. I was glad I'd been able to revisit the Arctic Circle; it reminded me that I needed to nourish myself with the light in the darkness. I would bring that rekindled Finnish spirit home with me, transferring it to my milder Atlantic island, if I could.

Whiteout, Blackout

In every walk with nature, one receives far more than he seeks.
– John Muir

At Upper Burbage Bridge, twenty miles from home, we – Tom, the two sons, and I – set out for Stanedge Pole on Boxing Day. It was not the North Pole, and we were not in the polar night. Instead, the Dark Peak was shrouded in opaque light, and the ground, still holding a residue of warmth, had yielded to patches of slushy snow. Jamie slipped on its icy covering and slid down a bank, and we all laughed. My family, complete and present for the first time since summer, was setting out to conquer the relative wilds of winter in Derbyshire.

There was a short, sharp climb up to Cowper Stone, a solitary gritstone rock with its pancake layers pouncing out of the fog. We climbed higher through rock debris, jumping from stone to stone, feeling the gritstone crunch beneath our boots – the sand, silt and gravel that had been washed up by the great deltas of the Carboniferous Period.

We reached the summit of White Path Moss and continued along Stanage Edge. We knew the rocks fell away sharply to the land below, but a curtain had come down. All we could see was the mosaic of black and white at our feet: dark rock, ghostly snow. Thin sheets of ice glossed the gritstone, and the pools of water were cloudy slush. The Finns have a single word for all of this: *loska*. We stumbled across the edge, the rocks slippery with ice in some places, the ground thick with mud in others. Our pace was slow, and the light was beginning to fade out. At last, we veered away from the edge to climb the Long Causeway towards Stanedge Pole. We were glad of the easy track, a medieval packhorse route that linked Sheffield with Hathersage. Some believe the trading route was once a Roman Road, and Stanedge Pole the meeting point of the ancient kingdoms of Mercia and Northumberland. The smudged light had taken on a pale grey sheen, and I wondered if the Roman Legionnaires, said to wander lost on Bleaklow to the north-west, had ever found their way here. It was not difficult to imagine ghosts as the light ebbed away.

On the edge of Redmires Reservoir, we headed across White Stones, the sweep of featureless moorland stretching out in front of us. Mud, slush and snow – *loska* – obscured the pathway and we found ourselves marooned in boggy land. I fell into a swamp, my boots disappearing into the mud.

'Oh, mum,' said Patrick.

'Oh, mum,' said Jamie.

And they were both laughing helplessly. I was laughing helplessly too, more in hysteria than anything else. I tried to pull my boot out of the mere, but it was firmly stuck. Patrick pulled at my arm, while Jamie tried to pull my leg out of the mud, only succeeding in leaving the boot behind. Several attempts later, the boot dislodged, my trouser bottoms and socks covered in peaty goo.

As the night gathered, we continued, jumping from tuft to tuft. Then, with relief, we saw a higher, bog-free path stretching arrow-straight to the road ahead. By then, we were completely enveloped in darkness, the light of my torch picking out the snow-lined path, the moorlands an unknown blackness beyond, the glow of artificial light from Sheffield a halo on the skyline.

There was something thrilling about being out in this semi-wilderness in the silence and cover of night. I felt its danger, I felt its adventure. Along with the phone GPS, we had a physical map and a compass, food in the rucksack and water. We just needed to tread carefully. Ahead, we could see the lights of other head torches: we'd reached Ringinglow Road. There was just the long march along its grass verge. Back at the car park, others emerged from the moorland, torches bobbing in the darkness. We were not the only night wanderers. Back home, I wrote in my gratitude dairy: *the thrill of the dark; the thrill of the light-giving snow; family silliness.* Like the Finns, I'd embraced the darkness on that Boxing Day night in the damp snow and peat of our Gulf Stream-tempered island.

January

In the Stillness

Be faithful in small things because it is in them your strength lies.
— Mother Teresa

January. A time of new beginnings and renewed goals. A time of expectation and hope. A time when we set ourselves up for a fall. January is the most difficult of months, especially for those who wrestle with Seasonal Affective Disorder.

While the Winter Solstice had come and gone, and the northern hemisphere was leaning into lighter days, the shift was minuscule, the stretch of days a crawl. Even though the light of the polar night had shaken me awake, I wanted to hibernate again. There were no sunlit, snow-bright days that had helped me through the previous new year. There was no Arctic Circle with its otherworldly polar night. My pulse slowed, and my brain felt sluggish again. *Same old. Same old.* Once more, I was reluctant to leave my bed, the quilt a comfort in the draughty house. I had to reel in my low mood in and reclaim the more positive narrative. My mind was full of doubt. Was it even possible to transfer the positive attitude of Laplanders during the polar night to our wetter, windier Britain?

I thought back to our Boxing Day walk in a slushy snow and mud of Dark Peak moorland and how it contrasted with the Arctic Circle. It was hard not to compare the winter conditions. I got in contact with Heidi, who had looked after our group in Salla. Heidi hailed from Helsinki and had spent years in Edinburgh.

'Is there a different mindset in Salla to Helsinki? How was that time living in the Arctic Circle for you?' After all, Heidi had spent a whole winter in Salla, not just a few days.

'I really enjoyed the winter in the north of Finland,' she replied. 'There is a different attitude to winter in Lapland compared to southern Finland. One of the reasons for this is that Lapland still gets proper winter with snow and cold temperatures.'

Heidi confirmed what I had been told again and again by local people inside the Arctic Circle.

'Bad winters in the south of Finland can be wet and dark with no snow. In Salla, the snow-covered ground really brightens the surroundings and makes everything look so much nicer in the dark. The light on the snow from the moon and streetlamps brightens the land and it doesn't seem so dark.'

I remembered the beauty of the Levi lake in the polar night, how bright the land and sky had appeared in the darkness. I asked Heidi whether she'd found it easier to slow down in Salla.

'Yes, definitely. Lapland winters give you the opportunity to bunker in. I felt no pressure to do activities in the evening, in contrast to summertime when it's light outside twenty-four seven. It's like the darkness gives you permission to take it easy, recharge the batteries, light the candles and be cosy.'

Downstairs, I lit the wood burner and continued to talk to Heidi. Along with lamps, candles, blankets and hot water bottles, the stove provided light, life, warmth and comfort. They were the moss lining my winter den. Here was something I could easily reproduce from Lapland.

'Is it harder to hunker down in Helsinki?' I asked Heidi.

'I don't get that feeling of bunkering in as strongly in Helsinki because it's just much busier in the city and there's more to do.'

'And what about the impression I got in Salla that life was spent outdoors, even in the polar night? Is that how it was for you?'

'Yes, it's true. In Lapland, many activities and hobbies happen outdoors. I loved the fact that you could see the sunrise and sunset on the shorter days. And finally, when the spring sun starts to shine after the polar night, you appreciate it even more after the perpetual twilight and darkness of winter.'

How true, I thought. And while the contrast in England wasn't as extreme as in the Arctic, living in the grey of winter meant I appreciated the colour, light and warmth of spring even more. I had felt that strongly last winter with observing the seasons more closely and spending more time in the outdoors.

'So, you didn't ever experience the winter blues in Lapland?'

'Never. It just gave me an appreciation of the more distinctive seasons there. In the Arctic Circle, you follow the dramatic changes in nature, and you are more aware of the rhythms of life. I have to say, the place I felt the winter blues most was when I lived in Edinburgh as the winters were dark and wet and windy – as they can be in southern Finland sometimes too. The dry cold and snow we get in Lapland is much better!'

I sighed. It clearly was more difficult to escape the winter blues further south, but I was not going to give up.

'Is it harder to get through winter in Helsinki and Edinburgh than inside the Arctic Circle?' I persisted.

'That's my personal experience. I do feel that people overall are more afraid of the dark season in the south than in the north. Maybe because people in the north are somehow more in tune with nature?'

Heidi gave some hope again with her last thought. I couldn't transfer the snow of Lapland to my home, but I would continue to engage with nature and the outdoors – it had already made a significant difference to my ability to get through the dark months of the previous winter, although I still felt I was on a journey of acceptance.

I thought about what Heidi had said about 'bunkering in' in Salla, remembering the online writer again who'd said winter is a time to slow down and reflect. This winter had been much milder and wetter than the previous one. My walks had, at best, taken me through half-frozen landscapes, ponds covered in the thinnest glaze of ice, patchworks of green and white where snow gathered in dips or sun-starved fields. On the worst days of rain, I read and wrote, taking pleasure from the smallest things: the heat of radiator-dried sheets on my face; stinging hot baths – the sensual pleasure of plunging my head under the water. Food provided warmth – hot soups, spicy stews, nuts, chocolate and sugar-packed puddings and cakes. In contrast, I loved the cold air on my face at nights when the winter winds blew through the open window.

Despite not having the bright snows of Lapland, there was much to love about my island winters. Night after winter night, year on winter year, I'd lain in bed and listened to our town's tawny owl, its quivering hoots ringing through the valley. In times of greater superstition, the call of the owl signified bad luck, even death. Some believed owls could steal your soul. Others thought owls were the only creatures able to live with spirits. I smiled to myself as I listened to their ghostly calls in the darkness. I could see why the link was made, but I found their calls oddly comforting. They were the soundscape of my small town, reassuring, always there. As far as I know, the tawny owl lives in a small woodland close to the town centre, but I'm not sure. I don't know if it's always the same one. I know its communication in the depths of winter is 'This is my hunting ground; steer clear.'

The sparrows also brought me joy in the colder months when birdsong is muted. Flittering from the hedge across our road to the bargeboard of our house, they were the sound of happiness. They flew right to the windowpane before swooping up to gaps in the wood. I was happy to share my home with them. I loved how they bathed in the street's puddles after rain, and how they chattered together. I loved their incessant chirping, how they wove through the cotoneaster with its bright red berries. I tuned into their energy.

I flicked through my journal record of that first winter, when I'd experienced the extraordinary in the ordinary of winter. There was so much joy in the smallness of winter life: a buzzard on the gatepost of a country lane; the kitchen window steaming up with cooking; the oven blasting out heat on opening; the smell of baked pies; Tom's soft breathing as he slept; the laughter of friends. The melt of an embrace. Without doubt, I was learning to love winter in the Midlands of England, even with all its ups and downs.

We continued our night rambles, Emma wanting to stretch our winter walks to summer lengths. Small things seemed large in the night of our extended walks. The detail of Derbyshire's topography, caught in the torchlight, fixed my attention: the glint of grit in stone, delicate patterns of moss and lichen and the snake and knot of ground roots. Sight restricted, hearing took precedence: small animal sounds, the sharp crunch of leaf and stone underfoot. The amphitheatre of the river's song in the darkness. Smell, too. The ozone of stream, the mulch of leaf, rotting vegetation. Wood smoke. The unnameable smell of night. Eyes widen in the darkness; child-sharp imaginings kick in again.

But in my adult mind, I was laid bare like the trees in January. I had to face the figurative darkness. Without the light, there were no distractions from my innermost thoughts. It rendered me vulnerable. It stripped me to the core of my existence. I asked myself *What is important? Warmth and shelter from winter's storms. Someone to support me through the darkness. Nourishment of body and soul. Breathing deep, absorbing the stillness, being present.* I wrote it down.

It was also time to take stock, reflect, re-evaluate and plan. *And dream.*

That winter, the kernel of an idea started to grow. I fantasised about the Trans-Siberian Railway that could take me right across the globe over ten time zones. And another journey from Vladivostok to Japan by ship. Through the month of January, books fed my fantasies: *A Gentleman in Moscow, The Lost Pianos of Siberia, Kafka on the Shore.* I started to plan. What would it be like to travel across the frozen steppe of Siberia to Japan in wintertime? How did the Russians survive the harsh, hostile conditions of Siberia at the turn of the year? I wanted to experience it first-hand. That dream would have to wait another winter – if the Russians didn't banish us over Ukraine.

But there were other places I could more easily plan for and reach within a few short weeks and escape the winter grey. And if Russia didn't work out, there were other frozen wastes.

Snowbirds

My soul is in the sky.
– William Shakespeare

At Christmas, friends had visited us bearing gifts: dried oranges, almonds and chillies from the foothills of the Sierra Nevada, the snow-covered mountains of Andalusia. The gifts were tucked into festive red sachets, brought from Phil and Michelle's smallholding. I hung the small presents of sunshine that had travelled from southern Spain on our Christmas tree.

Phil and Michelle had become snowbirds of sorts, a word used to describe North American retirees who escape the harsh winters of Alaska, Canada and the bordering States by migrating south to warmer climates – southern California, Florida, the Bahamas, Mexico and the Caribbean. They ape the great white birds of the Arctic and subarctic: Tundra geese, sandhill cranes, the black-tipped whooping cranes, American white pelicans and great blue herons.

Some Northern Europeans also migrate in winter to boltholes in the south of France, Spain and Portugal. Like the birds who stop short of Africa at the Mediterranean, Phil and Michelle migrate with the blackcaps and chiffchaffs to southern Spain after a few weeks in England, when they escape the heat of the Andulucian summer, and return a for the Christmas holidays.

The snowbird dream took shape on a bright June day in 2018 as Phil and Michelle sat on a balcony overlooking the Alhambra in Grenada with a bottle of red wine. Oblivious to the glowing pale red Islamic palace, its fortress and the snow-capped mountains beyond, they pored over a wine-stained piece of paper divided into three, headed 'must have,' 'nice to have' and 'extras to acquire.' The must have section sweetly listed 'Phil and Michelle', at least an acre of land, a structurally sound dwelling and a water supply for the house. In the garden, they had to have a variety of established fruit trees and *acequia* water – the dugout channels of mountain run-off that supply the *Cortijos* of the Alpujarra on the southern slopes of Sierra Nevada. In the nice to have section, they homed in on their ideal smallholding: lemon, orange, olive, avocado and nut trees; a woodland, kitchen garden with outdoor shower and wood burner, swimming pool, fishpond and an *alberca* – a water reservoir – and 'most importantly', a rustic eco-house. In the extras section, they added chickens, ducks, pig, donkey, dog and cat, and threw in a camper van and camping equipment for good measure – and a wish for permaculture knowledge. Phil and Michelle were dreaming the Good Life.

By July the following year, they had the keys to their *cortijo* with its half-acre *parcela*. They had found a traditional Andalusian farmhouse on the edge of Órgiva, suitably rustic with the required olive, fruit and nut trees. In the end, they had had to make do with less land than they had wished for, and the smallholding had cost more than they'd budgeted. But they had fallen in love with the whitewashed walls and sky blue doors of the old farmhouse, its covered courtyard, the swimming pool to cool off in on hot days, the bright skies, mountain air, and views of the high Sierra so close they felt they could reach out and touch them on clear days. Even better, Cortijo de Rosa – Rosa's Farmhouse – lay on the edge of a hillside town; they could step out of their *cortijo* into the countryside or walk to town in half an hour.

By the end of the year, Phil and Michelle had completed their first olive season, collecting 145 kilogrammes of olives to produce 21 litres of olive oil. With no previous experience, they had become *olivocultores* overnight. In the new year, Phil and Michelle blitzed the interior of the house, opening out rooms and letting in light, then pruned the long-neglected olive trees.

As for the permaculture methods Phil and Michelle wished for, they were in luck. Jey, the partner of Michelle's daughter Alex, was an expert. As Phil and Michelle returned home for spring, Alex and Jey moved in and watched the garden burst into colour. They built a birdfeeder, a lizard house and a bug hotel. The community farm took on new meaning: this was a parcel of land to share with animals and humans alike. Alex and Jey set to work, extending the irrigation system, recuperating the land and adding nutrients to the soil, building a lean-to planting station from recycled materials. They started to catalogue the foreign plants and trees in the garden so Phil and Michelle would know what they were and when they would bloom and bear fruit. They dug and planted and watered, and bit by bit the kitchen garden took shape. By May, the kitchen was filling up with the fruits of their labour. There were trays of drying apricots and oranges, stacked jars of lemon and orange marmalade, loquat chutney and 4 litres of loquat wine.

By June, the soil was regenerating nicely. The couple planted clover and other leguminous plants to make a green manure that would put nitrogen back into the soil. They added horse manure and wood chips, using only organic materials. The 'desert' land spread with wildflowers, attracting bees, the restored soil crawling with bugs. With grasses, chippings, manures and mulches covering the ground, the soil, protected from the hot sun, was able to keep its moisture. Tomatoes, peppers, basil, lettuces, kale, courgettes, squashes, watermelons, spinach and sunflowers all sprang up. By July, a wildlife pond had been added.

As I read these exuberant accounts from Alex, the sun outside my winter window split the pewter clouds, the rows of birches lined in wet light, the clouds separating and gathering then sailing away across the sky. Remembering the orange segments Phil and Michelle had gifted me, I ran downstairs. I'd taken them off the Christmas tree with the other decorations at the beginning of January and hung the sachets' drawstrings on the corners of picture frames. I drew an orange segment from the bag and held it to the light. The dried fruit glowed like beads of amber run through with veins. The sunshine of Andalusia shone through England's dull winter light.

I made a coffee and sat down with the orange segments, realising the 'browning edges' had in fact been dipped in chocolate. I savoured each bite: the tangy sweetness of the Andalusian sun, the crunch and chew of the fruit, pith and rind, and the richness of the chocolate. Each segment took me to Phil and Michelle's *cortijo*, to the high Sierra, to the mountains dusted in snow, to the little courtyard with its rustic dining table and chairs and the olive trees shimmering silver grey.

My gratitude diary read: *gifts, friendship, the beauty of far-away places.*

It was then, in the bleak midwinter of Derbyshire's January, I had the idea. I too could be a snowbird, if not for the whole winter season, at least for a few days. I messaged Phil. Would he and Michelle still be there at the end of February, the beginning of March? Could we come? Only if they were not too busy, if they didn't have any other plans. And we would be happy to help in the garden.

'It would be great to see you and Tom,' Phil reassured me. 'The weather should be lovely then. Malaga is only an hour and a half away, Granada an hour, and there are gorgeous mountain villages close by.'

I was giving in to the desire to escape our British winter. Was I giving up? What had happened to my resolve to change my mindset? But I was now yearning for the light and warmth of the Mediterranean. Derbyshire's winter could be exchanged for Andalusia's spring, the small things of England exchanged for the small things of Spain: bowls of olive oil, slices of citrus fruits, the gnarl and twist of olive bark, dusky grey-green leaves; the deep shadows of the mountains' folds, the savanna yellows of the foothills. And other still unknowable small things. All waiting.

February

Winter Storms and Almonds

We zagen hoe er vrede is, zelfs in de storm.
(We saw how there is peace even in the storm.)
– Vincent van Gogh

We drove to one of the highest villages in the Peak District, the upland settlement surrounded by fossilised medieval strips, small narrow arable fields enclosed by drystone walls in pleasing geometry. We halted the car on the edge of the village. The limestone houses were a snowy smudge outside the window.

'Let's wait for the storm to blow over before we set out on the walk,' I said, hearing the shame in my voice. 'We can eat our picnic in the car.'

We ate soup from a flask. The hot liquid steamed up the windscreen. Cottages and fields dissolved into water. It felt as if were on the high seas. The wind buffeted the car, whimpering and whining. Charcoal clouds rent to unveil a remnant of aqua blue, briefly promising brightness, then closed in again. Outside, sleet gathered on kerbsides before melting into the road. I stepped outside the car to take a picture of the highest church with a spire in England, a gilded locust balanced on a weathervane perched on St John the Baptist's slim steeple top. The heat of John's desert was impossible to imagine. A snow hare would have been more suitable, I thought grimly as I wiped sleet off my face. I was fed up, sick of the endless days of rain – and I was angry I was losing the narrative rewrite.

Across the road, the lamplights in the Church Inn's windows beckoned, but we were stuffed with cream of chicken soup from the flask, fruit, coffee and chocolate. The walk we had planned headed over the moorland before dropping down into a slash of dale, a deep scar in the belly of the White Peak. We'd have to climb the wall of Deep Dale (a different valley from the one we'd walked the previous winter), almost vertical in the slip of sludge and water.

The voice of the wind rose.

'I don't think I want to walk the High Peak in this storm,' I said. 'We could go to the Countryside Bookshop instead...'

Tom was quick to agree, and we drove on to a large, galvanised shed, books heaving on shelves, paper stars in the rafters. The door slammed back as we opened it and the wind whipped in behind us. We bought a book about Andalusia with pictures of spring flowers, a tumble of whitewashed mountain villages echoing the snowy summits of the Sierra Nevada. The sky was a block of blue in every photograph. Bright, bright, bright. I could feel Andalusia's warmth off the glossy pages.

Back home, Phil shared pictures of almond trees in Torvizcón from Spain: blue light, dabs of pink, dark twists of trunks, grey blur of distant mountain, moss green of foothill, straw yellow meadow.

'The almond blossom may be over by the time you arrive,' warned Phil. 'I think the blossom is a bit early this year,' then promised me there would be plenty of oranges and lemons, now ripe and falling off the trees. I remembered the sweet, sweet taste of Mediterranean oranges, so unlike the bitter, acidic offerings that made their way by ship to our northern island, picked too early.

The orchard pictures reminded me of the sachet of almonds Phil and Michelle had given us at Christmas. I opened the bag and poured the almonds out onto the kitchen table. They clattered across the wood; one larger nut unshelled. I cracked it open and bit down on it. There was a burst of marzipan flavour, strong, nutty, sweet. I'd never noticed this potent taste of almond before. I took out a packet of sliced almonds from the baking cupboard to see if my tastebuds had not registered the flavour before, but there was nothing. No taste. Just texture.

I took the remaining Andalusian almonds, spread them out on a roasting tin and placed them in the oven, then cooked up a sauce of olive oil and honey with a little sugar. Covering the roasted almonds in the sticky juice, I served them up in tapas bowls with sultanas along with ruby port and presented my gift to Tom. We closed the curtains, the wind an injured animal, rain thrashing the windowpane, and put another log in the wood burner. Andalusia spread over my tongue. I settled down with a book and blanket.

That February weekend, the storm raged on, howling and dying away before springing back to life. We ventured out to meet with Ian and Emma in their home, heads bent against the icy rain as we climbed the Bank. Inside, toasted French baguette slices covered in red and green pesto and olives warmed our bellies. More flavours of the Mediterranean: pine nuts, garlic, basil, chilli. Parmesan cheese. Wine.

Sue, Ian and Emma planned a walk for the following day but when it arrived, the wind was still buffeting the house, whistling through cracks, rising through the floorboards. Rain rattled the windows. I closed the curtains, lit the fire and sent my apologies. Later, Ian sent over pictures of the three of them – ragged, wet and grinning in a woodland, holding up flask cups of tea. *Cheers*, I said, curling up on the sofa.

What had happened to the lessons I'd learned from the Finns? I felt guilt. I felt I'd failed in my quest to love the rain and dark. And now I was planning an escape! But somehow it felt right to stay inside as the rain sheeted across our valley. The foxes, rabbits, badgers and birds knew better, hiding in dens and holes and hedges. Resting. Hibernating. And birds migrated south.

The Calm Between

Happiness makes up in height for what it lacks in length.
– Robert Frost

Still, I started to feel cabin fever. As the wind dropped and the rain and sleet eased off, I pulled on my boots and headed to Lea Wood, a steep-sided knoll of oak and birch, crowned with soaring Scots pines. The knoll looks like a Bruegel painting; I imagined it filled with birds and badgers, foxes, rabbits and deer – and hunters with game dangling from forked sticks. As I skirted the base of the forest, the sun stepped out from behind a cloud and brightened the way.

Soon, I reached the railway bridge crossing the River Derwent. A train thundered through and plunged into the tunnel cutting under the hill. Ahead, the chimney stack of the Victorian Leawood Pumphouse poked over the trees, built to pump water from the river to the canal. I emerged from the short arm of the canal at Aqueduct House. Florence Nightingale, who spent summers at the nearby country house of Lea

Hurst, reportedly visited the tenants living in the little canal house. Later abandoned, the roof had caved in, and the little house was all but ruined. Now, the cottage and its surrounds buzzed with activity. Men were felling trees. Hammering was ringing inside the building, which was now reroofed with new windows. I climbed the steps and backtracked along a higher path that ran parallel to the trail in the valley I'd just walked. The trunks of tall, spindly oaks were nailed with curious black metal boxes, each one numbered. Bat houses. Between the oaks, the barks of birches shone Scandinavian pale. There was no sign of foxes, rabbits and deer – or Bruegel-esque hunters – just the call of a coal tit.

I climbed higher through the woods, crossing a clearing. At the other end, there was a six-way fingerpost. Beneath it, I found my animals: badger, fox and rabbit crouched among toadstools under a thick canopy of oak leaves, all meticulously carved. Soon, the Scots pines I'd seen soaring in the sky from far below were just above me. Robin and blue tit added their voices in the stillness of the woodland. A blackbird scooted out of the undergrowth. As I emerged through the wooden gate of the nature reserve and out into the parkland of Lea Hurst, the sun came out again to bathe the backs of woolly sheep. I continued along the boundary of the country house on my solitary way. Florence Nightingale had loved her summers here. She'd written in a letter, 'It breaks my heart to leave Lea Hurst.' Dropping down along the eastern perimeter of the parkland, I could see why. Woodland and meadow fell then rose to the skyline, Crich Stand perched on top of a rocky cliff like a stranded lighthouse in landlocked Derbyshire. Florence didn't know winter here: the house was the family's summer residence.

She wouldn't have experienced the biting wind nipping my ears on the parkland height. Lea Hurst was forever summer, filled with gentle sunshine, soft rain and long days of light. No wonder she didn't want to leave.

I hurtled down the other side of the parkland, back to the canal. Florence may have taken this route to the Aqueduct Cottage. The towpath is caught between canal and river, the weedy water of the nature reserve between aqua blue and marine green. Even on dull days, the glassy canal reflects the beeches and oaks like a liquid mirror. Moorhens and mallards, trailing fluffy chicks, dive for weed, bottoms up. Below, the swollen river rushes east then south to Derby, singing its watery song, rapids glinting in the sunlight. Back home, I felt revived. A day of calm in the outdoors after the storms had restored my soul.

Winter medicine.

Winter Rains

Into each life some rain must fall,
Some days must be dark and dreary.
– Henry Wadsworth Longfellow

The rain fell. And fell. And fell. The sky was filthy. My mood was filthy. The land was muddied with water. To step out into this soggy world? But I felt trapped in the house. The walls were closing in on me. I needed out. I needed air. I needed nature's healing. Sod the rain! I remembered the previous winter, when I'd held my face up to the drizzle in Clough Wood and surrendered to it, promising myself I wouldn't let the showers hinder me from leaving the house. Was I backslid-ing? *Come on, Helen,* I told myself. *Pull yourself together. Snap out of this lethargy!* But it was *so* difficult in this wringing-wet weather. I gave myself a talking to. I'd step out with Tom, give myself up to the rain, even though the weather forecast had predicted heavy downfalls all day long with gusts of wind. I packed hot soup and coffee, and chocolate for comfort.

We set out through Tideswell Dale, passing a disused quarry of dark basalt rock. It was hard to imagine this place spewing lava and ash. Further down, paler limestone told another geological story: Tideswell once lay under warm tropical seas. I shivered in the damp rain and dreamed of coral atolls and turquoise oceans; my fingertips wrinkled with rain. Further down the valley, a wooden chair was inscribed with the words 'Ash Requiem 2021'. This landscape, once thick with ash and elm, was still changing.

My waterproof coat was already saturated, and the damp was seeping through to my clothes beneath. Alongside us, the swollen brook rushed its way to the Wye. We crossed the river, splashing through puddles on the path, and climbed the wall of the valley. Wet mud threatened to slide me downhill again. Tom grabbed my hand, wet on wet. On the exposed meadow on top, the wind pushed against our bodies and the rain came down so hard and cold it felt like hailstones. My eye sockets and cheekbones ached in the freezing downpour.

We took the farm track towards the hamlet of Priestcliffe, drystone walls luminescent lime in the rain-darkened sky. *At least the moss thrives in winter*, I thought. Just outside the hamlet, we took a sharp right, passing a farm with a burning brazier in an open-sided barn. The flames of fire were bright in the shadowy outbuilding, its warmth beckoning.

'Do you think we could slip in, dry out and have our lunch?' I asked Tom.

'Hmm. Maybe if the farmer had been around, we could have asked...'

Reluctantly, I walked on. The farm track had become a river and we were forced to squeeze along its narrow verges. We dived into the woodland, the path stepping steeply down through a tangle of trees, rock face and moss-covered stones. The woodland was a dead place of bare branches and a lifeless understory. Only the moss brightened the bone-coloured woodscape. We met no one, the hillside silent but for the patter of rain. Halfway down, we came to an abandoned den below a rock face where the land flattened out.

'Maybe there's enough shelter for lunch,' Tom said doubtfully.

We squeezed into the tepee-shaped shelter. Its creators had worked hard on its construction: three thick branches supported the structure, surrounded by thinner birch branches; even thinner hazel had been woven horizontally through the supporting branches. On top, the wigwam had been covered in moss, now disintegrating. The reindeer skins the Sami used to cover their *lavvu* would have been useful.

Tom poured soup. It was surprisingly dry in the shelter with just the odd splatter of rain plopping into my cup. How good the hot soup and coffee felt as they made their way to my stomach. Tom dipped his chocolate into his coffee, enjoying its warm melt in his mouth.

Down on the valley floor again, we followed a country lane that hugged the Wye. Dippers bobbed on rocks, disappearing into the rapids and flying from stone to branch and branch to stone. Mallards rested on the grassy banks. Great limestone cliffs rose from the river. It was a place of life-affirming beauty, even in the dulling rain.

Back home, I peeled off my sodden clothes, soaked in a hot bath, wrapped myself in radiator-warmed clothes and lit the fire. My cheeks flamed and warmth seeped through my body. My lungs felt stronger, my body tired and revived at the same time. Outside, the rain still fell, and darkness descended in the late afternoon. It had taken a day out in the wind and wet for me to appreciate the warmth of our dry Edwardian den, to feel life surge through my body.

Into each life some rain must fall.

An Arabian Gift in the Sierra Nevada

Mansas y turbias de penumbra yo sentía las canciones del agua.
(Meek and murky with the gloom I felt the songs
of the water.)
– Federico Garcia Lorca

We left our island for Spain, the sun rising with the aircraft, the sky blue-tinged white, red and gold spreading across the curve of the horizon, colouring the Midlands. We were escaping winter as the storms receded and the skies cleared. But in Andalusia, British-grey chilled the land.

'We're in desperate need of rain,' Michelle had messaged before we left. 'Perhaps you could bring some suitcases filled with water!'

'Only if you open the suitcases after we've left,' I joked.

While Derbyshire was saturated in rain, Andalusia had had a desperately dry winter. On the higher reaches of the

Sierra Nevada, the snow increasingly arrives later and melts earlier because of climate change. I asked Michelle if this was her experience.

'Yes. Definitely. The snow used to start falling at the beginning of October, continuing through winter. It would lie through spring and early summer, not completely melting until July. The last time I saw snow this late on the high Sierra was in July 2018.'

Snowmelt water – mountain run-off – is becoming scarcer, a disaster for wildlife, and the newly arrived *agricultores* from England. While I yearned for dry, sunny days, Michelle and Phil yearned for rain. The dark sky and weather forecast looked promising for them as we arrived at Cortijo de Rosa.

Still, Michelle and Phil laid the table on the patio: crisp lettuce, sun-ripened olives and tomatoes, beetroot, local *pan*, *queso* and *jamón*, lemon-flavoured water from the orchard, salad oil from one of their thirty-nine olive trees. Intermittent sunlight filtered through the gnarled branches of the vine-covered patio. Rosa the cat curled up next to the outdoor sink, waiting for the sun to warm her fur.

This was Andalusian winter. This was English spring. The sun coming and going. Patches of blue. Drapes of grey. A gentle warmth. A slight chill. It was a relief after the icy rain of home.

Phil showed us round the smallholding: the established fruit, nut and olive trees, the newly planted cherry, lemon and avocado trees, survivors of the previous harsh winter. The swimming pool was a tempting blue under the netting, but the sun had not yet warmed it sufficiently. The hammock field with our brightly coloured addition – a wedding present to Phil and Michelle – invited us to swing under the weak winter sun. The painted signs Alex and Jey made to demarcate the gardens had faded and peeled in the fierce heat of the Andalusian summer. The gardens were crisscrossed with the water channels they'd dug out. Water is precious here, essential for the organic food that fills the pantry and stacks the kitchen shelves, a quintessential part of the Andalusian *cortijo*.

That evening, Phil and Michelle showed me how to make *potatas a lo pobre* – Poor Man's Potatoes. Michelle covered the base of the pan with her olive oil, then she and Phil alternatively added layers of thinly sliced potatoes, green peppers, onion and garlic before drizzling more oil on top: a cooking *pas de deux*. As the stew simmered, Phil lit the wood burner, the dim room with its tiled floor, thick whitewashed walls and tiny shuttered windows bright in the orange flames. Warmth filled the house.

I could see why Phil and Michelle loved this life: the simplicity of growing their own food and cooking it, or shopping for local food, grown year-round; the healthy tiredness from spending a day in the gardens; their excitement in creating the *cortijo* of their imagination; belonging to the close-knit community of Northern European immigrants who were breathing life back into dying Alpujarra settlements.

Would moving to Andalusia be a solution for my winter blues? I could see the attraction, but something inside me held me back. Paradoxically, I was a northern soul. That night, I went to sleep to the sound of throbbing frogs and barking dogs. I wondered if I could ever grow to love Andalusia in the way Phil and Michelle did. I'd noticed in the garden that my eyes had been constantly drawn to the snow-topped Sierra Nevada; part of me was still in the Arctic Circle.

* * *

Over the week we spent at Cortijo de Rosa, a stream of tradesmen, itinerant labourers and migrants visited the small-holding: a Spaniard to quote for a solar system; an Irishman to plant up shrubs and trees; a northern Italian to prune the olive trees and let the light in. English neighbours dropped in, lending tools and offering gifts of food.

'Often, we'll arrive home after a day out to find a bag of food hung on the gate,' Michelle told me.

Tom and I spent mornings helping in the garden, sifting leaves from twigs and shredding branches for ground cover, cutting background shoots from the orange tree, shifting rubble, securing a fence screen, gathering oranges, juicing oranges, cooking a pasta bake and shelling almonds. The rain threatened but never delivered more than a few half-hearted spots, or sprinkles of light drizzle. On the Sunday, Phil and Michelle received a response to their request for water from the president of the *pozo*: they would receive it that evening at 5pm for half an hour.

'The *pozo*,' Michelle explained, 'is the well water that's released into the *acequia* when there's insufficient mountain run-off to reach this far down in the valley.' The *pozo* is an essential backup system for the *fuente* – the meltwater that's channelled all the way down from the high Sierra to the River Guadalfeo.

I thought of the rain back home and how I cursed it. But we didn't have to borrow from mountain run-off or ancient Moorish channel systems with village reservoirs as a backup. I remembered my Italian sister-in-law's mother's first visit to Britain. '*Verde, verde, verde,*' she said repeatedly with the wide eyes of a small child experiencing something for the first time. She couldn't get over the greenness of our island. On

Sardinia, where she was from, the green lasts through the winter months and early spring, but for the rest of the year, the landscape is hay yellow. We were blessed in the British Isles: winter green remained with us year-round. I needed to remember that.

Michelle and I set off to check the channels and grates at the top of the property.

'It's our responsibility to make sure the neighbours' grates are closed off, otherwise our water runs into their properties,' explained Michelle.

We followed the *acequia* – the flume of concrete – around the northern boundary of the garden, making sure the neighbours' grates were fully closed and that no stones were caught at the base of the metal, allowing water to divert away from Cortijo de Rosa. Everything was as it should be.

The *pozo* president messaged again.

'The water will be with you in five minutes.'

We waited. At first there was nothing, then a trickle, then a gush. The water raced through the channel, flooding the wildlife pond, then the vegetable plot. Michelle scooped up buckets of water from the *acequia* and I poured water around the base of the young cherry, lemon and avocado trees.

With rising temperatures through spring and early summer, the *fuente* is a lifeline for the parched olive, nut and fruit trees as well as the garden kitchen. This ancient system of irrigation, created by the Moors more than a thousand years ago, still sustains the farmers and gardeners of Andalusia today, the winter gift of snow providing much needed meltwater.

Foraging in the Alpujarra

Cada paso que damos en la tierra nos lleva a un mundo nuevo.
(Every step we take on earth brings us to a new world.)
– Federico Garcia Lorca

'I always try to remember to pack a bag and a trowel when we go out,' Michelle laughed.

We'd walked along the banks of the Guadalfeo, the water in fast flow. Above us, eucalyptus trees teetered on the edges of the eroded riverbank, roots dangling over our heads. We gathered twigs and bark for kindling. Michelle dug out wild herbs.

Phil had been right; the almond blossom was largely over. But as we left Órgiva behind to drive into the Sierra de la Contraviesa above Torvizcón, the orchards on the upper reaches were still in bloom. At first, Michelle gathered nuts on the dirt track, but then we found two trees that had been missed in the previous harvest (or perhaps had borne fruit later) still laden with almonds. We gathered a bag full, the Sierra de la Contraviesa dropping away to the valley below us, a world at our feet. White-squared farmhouses dotted the hillside, dust tracks winding through orchards, spines of roads on the crests of hills. The delicate pinks and whites filled the air with light, just as the snow had done in the Arctic Circle. Back at the house, Tom and I de-shelled the nuts and refilled Michelle and Phil's almond jar, squirrelling a bag into our suitcase. Back home, I would make more almond sweets to comfort us in the winter of England.

I found out more of Michelle's story. She'd felt the pull of Andalusia from that first winter when she'd discovered she could rent a place very cheaply. The Órgiva community welcomed her in. Michelle had found her spiritual home, far from her northern island, far from the bricks and concrete of London where she was from. She returned to Andalusia again and again, renting places across the township, some-times house-sitting. She dreamed of buying her own *cortijo* and settling permanently in Andalucia. I, in contrast, had come here for a short sojourn. I'd come to escape the rain-storms, the biting cold and dark skies. I'd come to find out what had fired their passion for Iberia. The Latin countries had never called to me: I'd been drawn to the icy winds of the polders and exposed wide sands of the Netherlands on the edge of winter; to the snow-covered Alps of Switzerland and the frozen landscapes of the Arctic Circle. If I felt the darkness of winter weighing down on me, why did I seek out the coldest and most exposed parts of northern Europe? It made no sense.

Now, I was seeing Andalusia through the eyes of Phil and Michelle. I absorbed their passion, their love of outdoor life in the garden, but I needed time alone so that I could take in the foothills of Sierra Nevada unfiltered. I slipped out of the house and down the lane, veered right past the goat farm, crossed the dried-out Chico River and climbed up into a valley where winter was slipping into spring. The sky hung low, the rain falling light and silvered. Here, the terraces that stepped down through the valley were a lush green, the first yellow buds of wildflowers soon to spread gold under the olive groves. The thick knotted trunks of the olive trees told me they were hundreds of years old. Across the terraces, elegant villas took shelter among poplars and pines. I met no one on the lane. There was silence intermittently broken by a cascading scale of chaffinch, a sweet phrase of a blackbird and a chatter of sparrows in bushes. This was a prologue to spring, not just in Andalusia but also at home.

Into the Blue

Todas las cosas tienen su misterio.
(All things have their mystery.)
– Federico Garcia Lorca

'This is the coldest it's been since we arrived here after Christmas,' Michelle admitted.

Before leaving England, Michelle had warned mornings and evenings would be cool, the heat building up through the afternoon.

'It's best to layer up, then layer down as the day warms up,' she advised.

But the air had remained stubbornly chilled under a lid of cloud on those last days of February, and we'd kept our fleeces on. Then, on the first day of March, we woke to clear skies.

We drove out into the blue, snaking our way along the Guadalfeo valley, ibex feeding on the verges. We stopped at Rules Reservoir at the confluence of the Guadalfeo and Izbor rivers, the sky above royal blue, the water beneath navy. The air was still, the sun a balm on the skin. I felt peace. I felt a coming to with the first spring buds of the Alpujarras.

We continued along the southern leg of the three-pronged triskelion that shapes the Rules Reservoir and into the ravine of Tayo Los Vados. The great limestone rockfaces either side of the Guadalfeo squeezed us through the mountains before spitting us out on the coastal plain. At Salobreña, Michelle and Tom hunted for flat smooth pebbles to take back to Órgiva: schists sparkling with garnets, slivers of slate and pale pink rose quartz. I walked alone towards Caleta-la Guardia, white, flat-roofed houses tumbling to the sea. The Mediterranean was a soft swish on the shore, the sea an intensity of blue. In the mellow warmth, I felt my muscles loosen and my mind float. How different it was from the wild Welsh coasts of the Marloes Peninsula where we'd walked a few months earlier. The energy of the North Sea and Atlantic Ocean, and the interplay of light and dark on the water, had made me feel vital and alive. These mellow days of Andalusia would reach us soon back home. And I would appreciate their light and warmth even more because of the cold and dark months of a British winter.

Later that day, we climbed up to the Castillo de Salobreña, the town at our feet, the distant snow-capped Sierra Nevada above the plains spread like icing sugar, the sea a sparkle. We dropped down the hill through alleyways of white, pots of bright colour against whitewashed walls, tiles of blue singing the ocean, voices bouncing off gables.

'*La poesía es algo que anda por las calles que se mueve que pasa a nuestro lado*' – 'poetry is something that walks the streets, that moves, that passes by our side', Lorca had written. I felt the poetry of the narrow streets below the fortress, bathed in blinding light. Costa Tropical.

Should Tom and I move here? I wondered to myself. *Was this not the answer?* Here, summers lasted near enough eight months of the year. I was guaranteed light. I was guaranteed warmth.

'You should go up onto the roof patio to see the sunset,' Phil said back in Órgiva. I climbed onto the sunroof and watched the olives and hills wash in orange light, the sky growing pale, the hills falling into shadow.

For a moment, I saw the Alpujarra of Phil's eyes. I fell into its winter-into-spring gentleness. This too would come to me in the Midlands of England. Instead of the pink almond blossom on the lower slopes of the Sierra Nevada, I'd look out to Masson Hill, yellow-bright with buttercups. I just needed to be patient.

The Red Palace of the Alhambra

Si lo que tengo bajo mis pies es el paraíso, ¿qué es la Alhambra?
¿Cielo? (If what is beneath my feet is paradise,
then what is the Alhambra? Heaven?)
– Lope de Vega

On the edge of Granada's medieval quarter of Albaicín, we drank our *cafés con leche*. The winter sun glowed on the Alhambra on the hill above us, the castle walls a warm salmon colour. The air was still morning-fresh in this high-level city flanked by the snow-topped Sierra Nevada. Those first chilly days of the Alpujarras seemed a distant memory, the sun now burning through my winter blues. What was it about sunlight that stills the mind? Once more, I felt at peace. Quietened.

The first written records of the Alhambra date back to 889 when Sawwar ben Hamdun took refuge in the existing fort. From then on, the site was extended, a castle added to the military fortress. But it wasn't until the arrival of Mohammed Al-Hamar, the first King of the Nasrid Dynasty (and the last Arabian dynasty of the Iberian Peninsula), in the 13th century that the Alhambra became the magnificent royal residence that inspires today. A watch and keep were added to the reinforced fortress and water canalised from the River Darro. Work on the palace and ramparts began, public baths and a mosque added. The castle city with its pools and gardens, glittering rooms and courtyards multiplied under the prosperous reigns of Yusif I and Muhammad V in the 14th century. Alhambra is one of Europe's most dazzling castle complexes.

In the Capilla Real, we paid our respects to the 15th century royal power couple, Isabella I of Castile and King Ferdinand II of Aragon, who'd unified Spain with their joint kingdoms. In the coolness of the Royal Chapel, I felt winter again despite the warm glow of the alabaster effigies, the royal couple regally crowned and gowned. But on the hilltop, sunlight poured through the Alhambra, geometric tiles the moss green of rain-washed valleys, the cobalt of summer sea and amber of sun. Courtyards of pools captured the sky and the rose-tinted walls of the palaces.

I thought back to the repeating patterns of the Lincolnshire coast: ripples in the sand, seabird feet, dune teasel heads and saffron on the foreshore, and how I'd been drawn to them. Later, I'd discovered our brains connect emotionally to lines, shapes and repeated geometric patterns. The psychiatrist Carl Jung recognised the importance of symbols on the unconscious mind. Architects design with an awareness of how we subconsciously react to lines and shapes visually and emotionally. We are drawn to the softness and fluidity of curves and circles; they soothe us. Straight lines and angled shapes appeal to us with their stability and order, the repeated patterns of geometry even more so. I didn't know whether the Moorish artists, designers and architects of the Alhambra knew the science behind the psychology of colour, line, shape, symmetry and repeated pattern, but they understood it at least instinctively. Nothing was left to chance at Alhambra. The courtyards provided shelter from the harsh Nevada winter winds and trapped the sun. The rows of paneless arched windows provided cooling breezes in the heat of summer along with the pools, fountains and greenery of courtyards. The Moors had made the best of all the seasons. I needed to do that at home as well.

The swirling patterns of writing on the walls hold subliminal messages that reflect the comforting order of the tiles and carved walls, ceilings and doors: 'Happiness'; 'Blessings'; 'Go in peace'; 'Rejoice in good fortune for Allah helps you'. Beneath the Arabic scripts, delicate filigree patterns echoed the floral patterns of nature. In this place of great beauty, I felt serene. I felt joy. I fell into Alhambra's beauty: the warmth of its intricately patterned cedar wood doors and ceilings, the swirling ivory plasterwork; the wave of arched columns reflected in the light-filled pools; the play of shadow and light; the soothing symmetry of plants; the rich reds, blues and golds of painted ceilings; city fragments caught in windows; gardens leading into gardens – Moorish symmetry colliding with the natural spread of spring colour. Beyond, the city of red roofs and whitewashed walls, snow blazed on the Sierra Nevada.

The Alhambra Palace was the last place to fall to the Catholic monarchs in the reconquest of Spain in 1492. This world could have been lost. When Isabella and Ferdinand moved in, they dismantled the mosque but largely left the palace intact. Their grandson, Charles I of Spain, however, in an act of pure vandalism, ordered the destruction of part of the complex to replace it with a Renaissance palace fit for a Christian king. Later, Napoleon attempted to destroy it but was thwarted by a quick-thinking soldier who removed the fuses. The Alhambra was all but abandoned in the 18th century, left to fall into disrepair. It wasn't until the 19th century that restoration began, continuing to this day – bit by bit, its treasures are uncovered.

And far from a dirty English winter, I received the blessings of this light-filled place of beauty.

The Green Gorge

Verde que te quiero verde. Verde viento. Verdes ramas. (Green, how I want you green. Green wind. Green boughs.)
– Federico Garcia Lorca

Phil and Michelle wanted to show us the *pueblos blancos* – the white villages of the Alujarras that spill off the mountains, appearing like patches of snow from a distance. We drove to the lower Poqueira Gorge and stopped off for *café mañanero* in Pampaneira. My head was still groggy, my sleep disturbed with anxious thoughts of the Ukraine war, my existential angst and the darkness that laid me bare again in the night with the barking dogs. But here in the *plaza* of this quiet village washed by cool mountain air and soft sunshine, my fears dispersed. My mind quietened and I fell into the moment: the rattle of cups, the muted blur of voices, the scrape of chair on cobbles, the tinkle of water splashing through a water channel in a *tinao* – the passageway above us.

The *pueblos blancos* are a maze of *tinaos*, narrow passageways of cobbled stone. We wandered up. We wandered down. We twisted around corners and found an open-sided building with great stone vats for washing, the green of the gorge calling through its arched windows. The Berber influence is still keenly felt in this mountain village, in the flat-roofed, whitewashed houses, in the tunnels of shops receding into shadows, in the clack of weaving from rug shops, and in the tall white chimney pots, spotlessly white or smoky black.

'They look like old men to me,' Phil laughed, and I saw what he meant – the drooping slits of eyes, the black caps and long thin white bodies.

We passed a *carnicería* hung with *jamón* and a rustic inn offering *carnes a la brasa* – grilled meats – its traditional wooden plaque painted with pink hams.

We followed a terrace walkway through the poetry of Lorca, the looping font on the signs reminding me of the joined-up script I'd learned (and forgotten) at school. We passed small windows, shuttered and grilled with one miniature window hung prettily with a blue and white macramé curtain.

On the long *terrao* of Lorco quotes inscribed into the terrace walls, an old man asked us for money. Phil offered him a coin and in return he gave Phil a shiny new screw. Across the Paseo de García Lorca, the mountains over the valley were green with trees and shrubs, the ground between dusted yellow with the dry earth of the Mediterranean. This mountain village had a simplicity and quietness that was healing. I could see why it appealed to town dwellers from northern

Europe yearning for a less complicated life. We continued to Capileira, the highest of the three villages in the valley. I wanted to walk on up into the narrowing gorge to Mulhacén, a two-day hike to the highest mountain in the Iberian Peninsula, and back into the snows of winter, paradoxically.

I felt confused. My mind calmed in the sunlight and came to in the harshness of the wild north. Winter seas fed me, windblown hills breathed life into me, cold and rain reenergised me, snow sang to me, sunlight calmed me. And there was the truth laid out in front of me – I needed it all: the gentlest of springs, the fullness of summer, the colour of autumn, the combined wildness and stillness of winter. I thought again of Takako's gift: the four seasons wooden dolls. Why were all four seasons so often depicted side by side in Japanese art and craftwork? Japan was known for its extreme winters and deep-piled snows in the north and central islands. I knew the Japanese sense of acceptance came from a deeply held belief in the need to find balance and harmony, both internally and externally.

The Finns had taught me the importance of living in nature, even in the depths of winter. They had shown me how to be comfortable in silence and to walk quietly in my own company. They had taught me the importance of communicating with nature, how to lose myself in the moment and become one with the external world. It had helped immensely – even though this last sodden January had been challenging at times. The nature bit was mostly easy – I felt an ease of spirit in the outdoors, but the slowing down, reflection and soul-searching still didn't come lightly. I had my demons I preferred to keep locked down; it was the only way I knew how to handle them. I wanted to push away the internal darkness instead of inviting it in. I would not allow myself to sit with it. But if I wouldn't sit with it, feel its weight in my hands, turn it over to examine its darkness from every angle, how would I ever find my way to the light? If only I could find a way to travel to Japan to experience first-hand their cultural and religious philosophy of gracious acceptance. It was a wild dream – the cost of flying across the world out of my reach. At least that's how it looked.

In the meantime, I would find ways to progress on my journey from darkness into light and back into darkness again, at ease with the rhythms of life.

The Third Winter

Across the World

October

L'été de la Saint-Martin en Bretagne

Expect Saint Martin's summer, halcyon days.
– William Shakespeare

The summer of 2022 was long and hot. Nights were spent on patios with friends under the glow of candlelight. My back garden was velvet-soft in the darkness. Bats swooped low over the patio table, leaving a quiver of air above our heads. We were drunk on laughter and music. We were drunk on wine and stars. I forgot the winter rains and embraced the blue stretching across a long spring and summer. At Easter, we'd walked the coast of Anglesey with Manuela (my Swiss friend yearning for the sea her country didn't possess), every day miraculously cloudless. Tom and I returned to Wales; we couldn't get enough of its coast. At summer's height, I'd explored the Isles of Scilly with my sisters and our men, the island air gentle, the lap of sea outside our tent pods a cradle song. I tried to imagine these offshore islands in winter, flung out into the Atlantic, and failed.

In September, Tom and I left for France with the camper. Despite all my efforts over the previous two winters, I was ambivalent about its impending return. The previous winter had tested me with its endless days of rain. And now, the summer, slowly winding down, had seduced me completely with its days of honey suns and nights of ivory moons. Hot days followed us down through Normandy and Brittany.

My face grew acorn brown. Life was spent in the outdoors, eating *en plein air*, cycling country lanes and walking rocky coastlines and long strands. I loved this Celtic coast with its gentle echo of our own Scottish, Welsh and Irish shores. I loved the shark-teeth islets and skerries, the mist-silvered bays and tall lighthouses that rose out of still waters.

September slipped into October. The rains came and went, offering up bright badger days in between. We spent the first day of October soaked in Roscoff sunshine, drinking coffee outside the *Café ty Pierre* with views of the harbour where the onion johnnies had crossed to England to sell their wares.

Days alternated between cool misty rains and steaming sunshine. We cycled through forests, past standing stones and dolmens and into fishing villages lined with seafood restaurants, the French tucking into large pots of seafood: mussels, cockles and crabs, lobsters and oysters, scallops and shrimps. Downing the sea. Downing summer. We followed snippets of the long-distance Brittany coastal path, picking our way round bays and headlands, the sun still fiercely hot.

But autumn was elbowing in. Days were warm but nights dropped in early and left a chill. The land and rivers smoked in the morning sunlight and inversion mists gathered in valleys. Beech nuts crunched underfoot. Leaves drifted down intermittently. Sweet chestnuts gathered on pavements. We watched the French strip coastal brambles of blackberries, comb beaches for cockles and mussels, and gather woodland mushrooms in baskets. These were halcyon days – the halcyon a mythical bird that breeds in a nest floating at sea at winter solstice, charming the wind and waves into calm. Those days in Brittany were the best of halcyon days.

But in Conleau and Vannes, we hugged the last hot summer day on the 11th of October before heading east along the River Loire. We had managed to bookend winter with an extended summer, first in Andalusia, now in Brittany. But I couldn't postpone winter indefinitely, could I? I looked back at my journal. I needed to prepare for the dark days ahead. I made a list: mindfulness, nature, forest, hill, sea, acceptance, gratitude. There was something else, however, something I had largely ignored over the previous two winters: I'd not dared to explore my darkest thoughts in the darkness of winter. This winter, I would dig deep. I'd face not just the physical darkness, but also the figurative darkness of my anxiety and fear.

L'automne sur la Loire

As imperceptibly as Grief
The Summer lapsed away.
– Emily Dickinson

I cupped my morning coffee in the blackness of the van, waiting for the light to come on. The little fan heater gave our doll's house on wheels a smidgen of warmth. In the morning chill, I pulled the curtains back, wiped away the condensation and watched the low light spread across the sky. The dawn eased in slow, night reluctant to give way.

The weather forecast informed us summer was coming to an end in Brittany. And so it was. The rain fell harder, leaves quickening their fall, dropping onto the campervan like confetti, clinging to the windscreen, gathering under the wipers, huddling together under the wheels in conspiratorial piles.

Upstream near Saumur, we visited the cave dwellings carved into the tufa limestone cliffs above the river. Troglodyte means cave dweller. The origin of the word is Greek: *trogle*, meaning hole, or mousehole, and *dyein* – to go in, dive in. I liked the idea of going underground, at least for winter. Tom and I felt like dormice in the tiny bed of our camper, curled up under the duvet, but when the light finally appeared we wanted to leave our mousehole – our cave – and explore.

We wandered passageways carved through the cliffs, natural rock reinforced by man-made arches and wooden struts. These cliffs edging the Loire have been occupied for centuries. Wine had been crushed under bare feet in cellars beneath the rock – the grapes thrown down a *jitte de pressoir*, a vertical shaft. Shelves in the rock had been occupied by troglodytes. We climbed up through underground passages to the vineyards. I slipped a bunch of grapes, missed in the harvesting, into my pocket. I ate them like sweets: a burst of summer sugar. Back down in the valley below the limestone cliffs, Tom gathered walnuts from the pavement, and we nibbled on grapes and nuts as we returned to our own nest on wheels.

As we continued upstream along the Loire, green was slowly surrendering to rusk, burnt orange and mustard. The colours seemed to offer themselves up to me as an appeasement for what was to come. Their brightness lifted me, but I knew what they signified: winter was cold on autumn's fiery heels.

The intensity of light and colour 'As imperceptibly as Grief – The Summer lapsed away', wrote Emily Dickinson. I felt her words.

All along the Loire, streets were emptying and restaurants shutting down. Proprietors left scribbled notes to say they were off *en vacances* – to somewhere warmer, no doubt. Tables and chairs were stacked up on terraces, the sun buried in grey, the light suppressed on its dimmer switch, days ebbing away into darkness.

But when the sun burst through, trees and grass became lustrous, the light and colour all the more intense for its briefness. And every day was new. Each corner rounded offering a landscape unseen before. I clung on to our French sojourn like the last leaves of the Loire clinging on to the dying days of summer. On the road, I was distracted by the beauty of France's coasts and rivers. At home, I would have to face the darkness.

Hot Leaf Walks

Our Summer made her light escape Into the Beautiful.
– Emily Dickinson

Everything has its end. Everything has its beginning. A new winter awaited me. I stepped out into the White Peak's edge of winter and left the Monsal Trail to climb up between limestone walls. The moors drifted across the skyline, the lines of escarpments dark brush strokes on the Peak District canvas. But I was dragging my feet. I didn't want to be out; I didn't want to be alone after six weeks with Tom in our mousehole camper. What happened to that psychological shift from the two previous winters? Once again, I had to relearn the lessons. I reached the brow of the hill and my mood lifted. It was good – the air cool but not cold, the land a flow of autumn brightness. Bakewell town lay below me, floating in orange. I tumbled off the hill and into town, racing the afternoon before the early dusk gathered, Emily Dickinson's words accompanying me as I climbed up to the trail again.

A Quietness distilled
As Twilight long begun,
Or Nature spending with herself
Sequestered Afternoon —
The Dusk drew earlier in —
The Morning foreign shone —
A courteous, yet harrowing Grace,
As Guest, that would be gone —
And thus, without a Wing
Or service of a Keel
Our Summer made her light escape
Into the Beautiful.

And on that walk, I yielded – once again – to the turning of the seasons.

November

Dreams of Japan

Solvitur ambulando. (It is solved by walking.)
– Saint Augustine

'If you kept on walking in this direction over the ridge,' Richard pointed with his litter-picking stick, 'the next high land you'll reach will be the Ural Mountains.'

I was standing on top of a remnant moor above Ashover, an island of heathland surrounded by fields that fell away to the plains. Richard was just one of the friendly strangers I met on my walks.

'You'll cross the North Sea, the lowlands of Denmark and the Baltic Sea,' he explained. 'At Moscow, you'll say goodbye to Napoleon then head for Siberia and the Urals.'

I liked the idea of walking crossing my continent to the next high land on the edge of Asia (disregarding the small matter of walking on water). I was still mourning the lost opportunity to travel the Trans-Siberian railway across Europe and Asia to Japan – cheap as chips on the local's trains across vast frozen wastes, making tea from the on-tap hot water, living off pot noodles, trying to decipher the Russian script and many time zones. Having made the journey in my head, it would have to suffice. I had been tantalisingly close to Russia in Finland, where the idea had taken root. How quickly world events unravel plans; first Covid, now

Putin's war. The invasion of Ukraine and the breakdown of Russia's fragile relationship with Europe had wiped my dreams away almost as quickly as they had appeared. There was also the Ukrainian community who found themselves washed up in my small Midlands town. They'd become friends. Even if I could have travelled across Siberia, would it have been right to do it?

As October tumbled into November, I eased back into my solitary rambles, watching pale golds and reds darken to spice. As I climbed up through Manners Wood between the Haddon and Chatsworth Estates, the larches sang with colour, their needles soft underfoot. I lived in the forest moment: the comfort of tree, the strength of trunk and root, the lullaby of silence. Here, in this mixed wood of oak, beech, birch, fir and larch, the trees drew me into their hug, obscuring all horizons. I felt at one with their intimacy.

Turning a corner, I reached the woodland's boundary. The world opened out to a valley of green, the echo of beech and stone wall an orderly march across the opposite valley. In the far distance, I could see the Chatsworth Russian Cottage tucked under moor and woodland, so incongruous in this quintessential English countryside of landscaped estate and upland heath. It was as close as I was going to get to Russia for the foreseeable future.

All these thoughts – past and future longings, the *fernseh* of my mind – were at odds with walking mindfully in the here and now. In all honesty, this was the nature of my walks. Often present, occasionally distant. I remembered the winter enthusiast who saw the season as a chance to take stock and re-evaluate. Walking in the low light of winter also gave me the chance to s*olvitur ambulando* – to work things out. Travellers Patrick Leigh Fermor, Bruce Chatwin and Paul Theroux were all great believers in *solvitur ambulando*.

The Trans-Siberian journey was beyond my reach, but Japan? The letters and gifts from my pen pal had drawn me in to her eastern culture, so different from my own. And now I was learning that Japan was not just the land of forest healing, it was also the land of *wa*. *Wa* – harmony – sits at the centre of Japanese culture, a philosophical approach to living in which the Japanese seek to lead a balanced life with everything in harmony. It influences everything they do, from their relationships with people and nature to the gardens they create and nurture, even the food they eat and how they prepare and present it.

It's unthinkable that a Japanese person would claim to prefer one season over another or talk negatively about winter. In Japan, the seasons complement each other. In winter, plants rest in preparation for renewal in spring. The buds and shoots of spring give way to the fruits and flowers of summer. The season of harvest gives way to the season of rest and renewal – and life's cycle starts over again. Each season yields willingly to the next – the harmony of nature – and in Japan, they are marked by countless customs, festivals and celebrations. The four seasons guide the Japanese through the year. The melting of the snow in the mountains, revealing the dark shapes of stone, is a sign for farmers to prepare the ground for spring planting. The cherished cherry tree blossom – so fleeting – is not a reason to mourn, but rather to celebrate life's transient beauty. Summer's bountiful harvests bring about a riot of celebratory festivals. Autumn foods are savoured: chestnuts, matsutake mushrooms, apples and grapes. Winter's celebrations light up the darkness with lantern parades and snow festivals.

In harmony with nature, the Japanese are not just in tune with the changing seasons but also the transitional periods between them. On the highest peaks, snow falls early. Below the snowline, the forested hills are still spreading autumn colour while valleys are green. The Japanese call these layers of seasonal colour *sandankōyō*.

As I scrambled down the gravel lane of Calton Lees, the easy sound of brook somewhere behind the hedge, I realised that Japan could help me to accept the inevitable arrival of winter on my journeys, and more than that, to welcome it in.

Reaching the flood plains of the Derwent Valley Heritage Way, I could see the upper branches of the larches on Beeley Plantation were already losing their needles, but as the sun momentarily came out, the conifers took on a radiance, a fiery brilliance that touched the core of my body. Everything changes. Russia was lost to me, but Japan had much to teach me. There was so much more I wanted to find out about Japanese culture, the way they gave equal regard to all four seasons, and why SAD is almost unheard of there. Reading about Japan was one thing, but what if I could experience the culture of *wa* first-hand? For decades, I had thought Japan out of reach – too far, too expensive – but tiptoeing through a churned-up farm track covered in runny cow manure outside Rowsley, I formulated a new plan. I would approach JNTO, the Japanese National Tourism Organisation, for a press-funded visit. I would need a commission. There were no guarantees – but wasn't that the Zen of Japanese belief? I would not worry about the things beyond my influence. I would put the wheels in motion, set out on the journey and see how far it would take me.

Washoku – Cooking in Harmony

L'art est une harmonie parallèle à la nature.
(Art is a harmony parallel with nature.)
– Paul Cezanne

It happened quickly – the press invitation and commission. A food magazine accepted my travel pitch focused on the Japanese art of harmonious cooking. I realised I knew precious little about Japanese cuisine apart from sushi and occasional Japanese meals cooked for me by Gill. I decided I would cook a meal for her this time. Traditionally, the Japanese use fresh, seasonal produce, and meals are prepared with nutritional balance in mind. The magic number is five. A balanced meal should, at least in theory, include five colours – green, red, yellow, black and white; five flavours – salty, bitter, sweet, spicy, sour; and the dishes should be prepared in five ways – raw, fried, simmered, steamed and grilled. Embracing all three elements of five was too daunting, so I decided to focus on colour. Gill agreed to bring the soup course. I would prepare a starter and main course. I made a marinade for a Japanese salad with soy sauce, sesame seeds, wine vinegar, sugar and salt. I found small bowls bought from the Grand Bazaar in Istanbul – Turkish in design, not Japanese, but at least small and delicate. I prepared cucumber and tomato dishes with the sauce and added a ball of Jasmine sticky rice in a third bowl. I had green, red, white and black (from the dark soy sauce marinade) but failed to add yellow.

Gill's soup tasted more authentically Japanese. At home, she'd cooked chicken in a teriyaki marinade with long delicate mushrooms she'd found at Chatsworth.

'Shiitake mushrooms are best,' she said. 'Or *enoki*, if you can find them.'

She'd added tender baby leeks, spring onions and green beans to the chicken, then white miso paste, giving the soup a cloudy appearance.

'So, what do you say before you eat?' Tom asked.

Gill placed the palms of her hands together, bowed her head slightly and said '*Itadakimasu*.'

This phrase simply translates as 'let's eat' but it's laden with meaning. It acknowledges the harmony between nature and man – from the fruits of the land and sea and the fisherman and farmer harvesting them to the cook who prepares the meal. It's grace stripped back.

I made my stir-fry, and we drank white wine instead of sake. I could only find one chopstick, so we made do with knives and forks. I had some way to go to successfully create *washoku* – harmony in food. I'd created four colours, I had achieved five flavours: saltiness, spiciness, sweet and sourness, and bitterness with the vinegar I'd added to my salad dressing. In my methods of cooking, I'd only managed raw and frying.

As we savoured Japan, the kitchen windows steamed up and our faces grew red from the central heating we sparingly used now because of the energy crisis. Every winter now, it seemed, had a new challenge. But every challenge, I realised, brought opportunities.

The Edge of Winter in Gifu

The wind howls but the mountain remains still.
– Japanese proverb

Over the Land of the Rising Sun, dawn bled across the arc of horizon. Below the aircraft, wisps of mist smoked off cedar mountain ridges and poured through valleys. There was something ethereal about this land, even viewed from high in the air. On the bullet train to Hashima, Mount Fuji rose from the plains like a child's drawing – a perfect cone dipped in snow, inky green below. The mountain was reassuringly solid and permanent , sometimes hidden by cloud, but always there. Nineteenth century artist Katsushika Hokusai thought differently as he created his print series *Thirty-Six Views of Mount Fuji* (adding another ten for good measure) through the four seasons. The block prints include his world-famous painting *The Great Wave Off Kanagawa*. In the foreground, there's a peak of wave, but it's overshadowed by a monstrous rogue wave, clawing the air like a wild animal. In the middle ground, the three curved bows of barge boats echo the curves of waves, almost merging with the seascape, while a small Mount Fuji in the background echoes the peak of the wave at the front. The tsunami-like wave threatens to swallow the barge boats, while the seemingly 'eternal mountain', appearing as a shape-shifting wave, loses all sense of permanence. After all, this volcanic mountain, erupting somewhere between 400,000 and 100,000 years ago, had almost buried old Fuji in its entirety as it rose from the lava. The *wabi-sabi* of Japanese culture – the acceptance of transience and imperfection – was something I would encounter again and again on my trip. Nothing is permanent, not even the great mountains that have stood for thousands and millions of years. The volcanoes, tsunamis and earthquakes in Japan stand testament to that, the violent activity of nature constantly changing its landscapes and cityscapes, threatening all life in its wake.

I realised it was foolish to strive for perfection, and yet I continued to do so. I yearned to be better, stronger, brighter, happier. I yearned to be the perfect mother, wife, sister, writer. It was all foolhardy. I failed at every turn. Somewhere deep in my subconscious mind, I knew that to be human is to be imperfect. Somewhere deep in my subconsciousness, I knew I needed to embrace the imperfectness of the world I inhabited, both inside and out. Gill had told me about *kintsugi*, the Japanese custom of mending broken ceramics and china with gold – the beauty of the imperfection. *Wabi-Sabi*. And deep down in the darkest part of my mind – although I had yet to bring it to the light – I knew that existence is not permanent and neither is mood. I still had to learn that I would continue to travel through winter with ever-changing moods – the landscape of my mind in all its light and shade, just like winter itself.

As the bullet train curved round Mount Fuji, the view felt unreal. Here I was, in Japan – a place that had occupied my dreamscapes – looking out at Japan's most iconic landmark in real time. My brain was fuzzy from lack of sleep, but the thrill of seeing Mount Fuji made me leap out of my seat, run to the window and exclaim with the wonder of a child.

'We're lucky to see Mount Fuji,' Naoko, our interpreter, smiled. 'The mountain is only visible around 20 per cent of the time.' Was this a good omen? Could Japan teach me *wa*?

Would it reveal its grace and beauty on the edge of winter –
a balance of all things in me and around me? Could I learn
to embrace the transition between autumn bright and dark
cold without having to relearn the lessons every single year?
Could I learn to love autumn's letting go and winter's retreat
as much as I loved the renewal of life in spring and summer?
Could I learn to accept the transience of life?

Outside the train window, Fuji's summit was winter white,
autumn spreading through trees on the lower slopes, the end-
of-summer rice fields yellowing on the plains. My anxious
mind stilled as I took in the mountain, its solitude, beauty and
simplicity of form.

That night in Gujo Hachiman, I walked the town as the
light gave out, the hills blackening, sky and river flushing pink,
the wooden castle with its curled and layered Japanese roofs
pale on the wooded hilltop. The sound of River Yoshida, the
fountains and streetside water channels were amplified in the
darkness. Fat koi carp circled the water. In the old days, the
townspeople had washed their vegetables, rice and laundry
here in the streets. Away from neon-lit cities, these ancient
mountain settlements in Gifu are steeped in tradition.

I wandered through the town, mist and dusk erasing the
river and hills surrounding it. The streets were empty but for
the occasional shadowy figure hurrying through. I felt out of
kilter in this utterly foreign place, where few people spoke
English. And alone. It was time to meet up with my fellow
journalists again in a local restaurant.

'Kon'nichiwa', I greeted a woman outside the doorway hung
with banners, unsure whether the indecipherable Japanese
script on the fabric corresponded with the English name on
my phone. I pointed to the restaurant on the map.

'*Hai, hai,*' she said, bowing slightly, pleased she was able to answer in the affirmative. '*Hai, hai*' –sometimes '*hai, hai, hai, hai*' – would become a familiar sound on my trip. For the Japanese, affirmative answers ensure harmony. The word 'no' is seldom heard.

'*Arigatō,*' I said, pressing my hands together and bowing in the Japanese way. I'd exhausted all three words of Japanese I knew, but we continued our conversation, the woman in Japanese, me in English, body language our shared means of communicating. She clapped her hands with excitement as I mimed kicking a ball and said 'Nihon' – Japan having gained an unexpected win in the World Cup. I clapped too. We laughed, two foreigners, not knowing each other's tongues, making a connection. And, in that moment, I felt less alone.

Pushing through the fabric banners, I ducked under the low door of the restaurant entrance. The darkness followed me into an intimate space of oak wood and low light. My fellow travellers and I removed our shoes as instructed before being taken to a small room with cushions scattered round a low table. Our food came on trays, the small bowls a kaleidoscope of colour: dark miso soup and seared Hida beef, snow white sticky rice and fermented fish, the summer orange of persimmon fruit and the reds, yellows and greens of autumn salad ingredients. A harmony of food, local and seasonal. Everything about this mountain settlement exuded *wa*: its food; its lullaby of running water; the cocoon-like dining-room of the inn; and the muted colour palette of The Oak Gujo, where I was spending the night – its dark polished wood and creamy paper *washi* screens diffusing light. Winter was presented to me as something intimate here: snug, womb-like, comforting.

As I journeyed through Gifu, I learned more Japanese words, most of them beginning with *wa: washi* – Japanese paper; *waka* – Japanese poetry; *wafuku* – Japanese traditional clothes; *washoku* – Japanese cuisine, and *washitsu* – traditional Japanese rooms, and *wabi-sabi*, of course. At its simplest level, *wa* means 'Japanese style' but traditional Japan embodies the concept of harmony. The two are synonymous.

The mountain roads led us to the *onsen* town of Gero and Ryokan Suimeikan, a sprawling spa hotel perched on the banks of Hida River. Despite the hotel's size, it had the intimacy of the small traditional Japanese inn – the *ryokan*. My room contained all the elements of the *washitsu*: *tatami* mat flooring, a low table and legless chair, *washi* screens and a raised platform adorned with a simple Japanese flower arrangement and off-set painting...but curiously no bed. As in Gujo Hachiman, the muted colours of the room and the uncluttered décor calmed my mind. The soft palette of dark woods, pale *washi* screens and sliding wardrobe doors echoed the mist-softened darkness outside.

When I had settled into my room, my *nakai* – maid – came in, knelt, pressed her palms together, bowed and ceremoniously welcomed me with green tea. She explained the three sets of slippers were provided for the bathroom, balcony and the rest of the hotel with its indoor and outdoor baths and Japanese gardens. She showed me my private bathtub, and my *yukata* – a light cotton *kimono* she instructed me to wear for dinner with the slippers in the entrance area. I wanted to giggle at the idea of going to dinner in my bathrobe in this high-end hotel.

I asked Naoko why. 'After everyone has been to the baths, they feel relaxed and the last thing they want to do is get back into their daywear,' she said.

Of course! How sensible. The *yukata* and slippers I wore
to our personal dining room were comfortable and relaxing
after a long soak in my *onsen* – and I was grateful for the
looseness of the wrap-over robe after a ten-course meal
with an array of colourful side dishes. Back in my room, I
discovered the *nakai* had laid out my futon for the night with
a thick duvet. Outside, mist rose from the river, the town
disappearing in the fog. I cocooned myself in the bedclothes,
the warmth, hot bath, colourful food and heavy duvet the
perfect antidotes to Japanese winter.

As we waited for our minibus to take us deeper into the
foothills of the Japanese Alps, I asked Naoko if she had come
across SAD. Lost in translation, Naoko thought I was asking
her if she was ever sad. She must have thought It a strange
question. I tried to explain what SAD was, but Naoko looked
blank. It was something that lay beyond her experience.

* * *

As we headed yet deeper into the mountains of Gifu Prefecture, I learned the natural world doesn't just teach the
Japanese the lessons of *wa* but also *mujo* – all things *must*
change. As I was finding out, nowhere is the unpredictable
power of nature's force felt more keenly than in Japan. the
changing of the seasons, humans, animals and plants die,
returning to the earth. Yet the Japanese have a deep love
and respect for nature, its ephemeral beauty celebrated in
the cherry blossom festivals. Coming to terms with the transient nature of life had never been easy for me. Japan was
encouraging me to further explore their cultural philosophy
of acceptance.

Our hosts took us to Gandate Park, a place where nature is both feared and revered. The hulking vertical outcrops at the entrance to the park are scraped and scoured by lava flow. Fifty thousand years ago, rivers of molten rock forged new valleys and river systems, radically changing the shape of the landscape. In 2014, volcanic activity caused havoc again. Mount Ontake, high above the park, erupted unexpectedly, killing fifty-eight trekkers, five of them never found Still, the Japanese continue to come here to trek and find healing in the ozone of waterfalls and the forested ravines below the volcano's slopes.

In the park's carpark, we took in the lava-scoured out-crops and clambered over the Japanese red bridge in the ravine below one of the waterfalls. On the other side, a warden had recorded the day's temperature and the number of negative ions in the air.

'The negative oxygen ions from the waterfalls,' the ranger explained, 'give us energy and make us feel refreshed. We've counted over 200 waterfalls in the park, and that's not includ-ing the smaller rapids.'

I wanted to explore the higher waterfalls and climb to the mountain hut below the volcano where Mo Farah had trained for the Olympics. But this was enough in this moment – just as I'd realised on the height of Masson Hill with Patrick. I breathed in forest. I breathed in the spray of the waterfall, the rot of leaves and the purity of mountain air. I felt at peace in nature and simultaneously invigorated by it.

Gandate Park is a wild and unpredictable place, a place where nature cannot easily be tamed. This was true, I was discovering, for much of Japan. Over 70 per cent of the country is covered in mountains. Its geographic isolation, lack of natural resources and inhospitable terrain has made it necessary for farmers and fishermen to work together to survive. *Wa* isn't just a desirable state of harmony for communities; it was born out of necessity.

I saw this as we travelled into the isolated settlements of Shirakawa-go high in the mountains of Gifu Prefecture. The recently blasted tunnel has brought the rest of the world to the Cultural UNESCO World Heritage Site, high altitude settlements that had been cut off from the rest of the country for centuries. In this remote area of mountains, village farmhouses look enchanting with their steeply pitched thatched roofs, almost extending to the ground. They are called *Gassho*-style houses because they have the appearance of fingertips touching as hands come together in greeting, prayer or gratitude in the Eastern tradition of *wa*. But *wa* goes beyond the appearance of these 'houses at prayer': they epitomise the traditional Japanese way of life, Shirakawa-go inhabitants working together in a hostile environment. When one of the *Gassho* houses needs rethatching, the community work collaboratively on the roof. It's this working together in harmony that has earned Shirakawa-go Cultural World Heritage status.

We'd arrived in Shirakawa-go after dark; our group split between three *ryokan* homestays. Naoko and I were dropped off somewhere in the higher reaches of the settlements. I shuffled down the long, lacquered corridor in my slippers to a room with an outside *washi* window, nothing between me and the chilled mountain air but thin paper. The house was cold – even colder than my Derbyshire stone-built Edwardian house – and the deep snows were still to come. I couldn't imagine what it would be like to live there in the depths of winter. I warmed up in the deep *onsen,* then went to dinner with Naoko. The lady of the house, the *okami,* her hair tied back in a scarf, came with our trays of dinner: rice from her own plot of land, a grill for the Hida beef and tofu, and plates of soup, fish and vegetables – dishes that just kept on coming and coming. The fire pit in the centre of the room barely kept the chilled air at bay. Later, the *okami* knocked on my bedroom door with a hot water bottle and asked me to switch off the gas stove. As soon as I switched it off, the temperature dropped several degrees, the clammy air outside seeping through the thin paper. It was hard to imagine why these mountain folk felt paper was a good window material in the snow that came every year and lay for weeks. *Is the chill going to keep me awake?* I wondered, but sleep came fast after the heat of the *onsen* and the many plates of food.

I woke in the pre-dawn, my body clock still not in sync with Japan, and climbed up through lanes of *gassho* farm-houses, homestays and barns in the spreading light; small, terraced rice fields squeezed into the sides of the valley. I felt all at sea in this foreign country, so culturally different from my own or indeed any other place I'd ever visited. The lack of sleep was making me anxious. One minute I was soaring high, the next feeling lost and overwhelmed. The extremes of emotions were exhausting. Then there were healing moments when I was quietened by the beauty, grace and gentleness of Japanese culture.

As I climbed higher, I saw the rice plants were withering in the muddy water. Soon, the heavy snows would come, covering the thatched roofs in a deep layer of snow. Down in the village, wooden boards had already been set at an angle against the sides of flimsy houses to protect them from the weight of snow. In this place, farmers have learned to live alongside the harsh winters. After the snowmelt, they come together to plant the new rice crops. But here on the cusp of winter, they were hunkering down. Waiting it out. All things in harmony.

On the Sea of Japan

To everything there is a season, and a time to every purpose under the heaven.
– Ecclesiastes 3:1

In Kanazawa, the snows hadn't yet arrived, but it wouldn't be long. In Kanrokuen Gardens, one of the three great gardens of Japan, the *yukitsuri* were already in place – the wigwam of ropes that surround the evergreens, protecting them from the weight of heavy snowfall. It was hard to imagine the frozen winters of Kanazawa on this bright late autumn day, the Japanese maples and cherries flaming reds and golds.

From the garden, we crossed to Kanazawa Castle Park and Gyokusen'an Rest House. The floor-to-ceiling window of the tearoom looked out to a red Japanese bridge reflected upside down in a glassy pond cradled by cliffs and autumn trees, incandescent in the sunshine. We were here to experience the Japanese Tea Ceremony, a tradition dating back 350 years when the samurai lord of Kanazawa brought a tea master from Kyoto to teach him the art of *chado*, 'the way of tea'. It quickly spread to the townspeople. *Chado* encompasses four essential qualities of Japanese living: *kei*, respect; *sei*, purity; *jaku*, elegance and tranquillity – an appreciation of the fleeting moment and renewal – and *wa,* the desire for reciprocity both in the teahouse and in the world.

I felt all of these in Gyokusen'an Rest House. I was quietened by the unhurried performance of my server, who lowered herself in humility and service. The detail of the ritual drew me into the moment – the stillness of the room and the beauty of the garden outside. The anxiety of my mind fell away. Before offering the frothy *matcha* green tea, my server knelt, bowed, then reaching out with two hands, she offered me a *Toraya Manju* sweet, a sugared bean ball made of sake, its covering of white representing winter snow. My server humbled me with her gentleness, the flow of her movements as she served the *matcha* tea a graceful dance, a formality of shape and form and transition of movement as precise as a ballet dancer's. I could see that her every movement was considered and exact – carefully and meticulously carried out. The lack of sleep was making me feel unusually tearful. The ceremony drew me in and drew from me something I didn't quite understand, something buried deep within.

Later, Naoko told me she was taking tea ceremony classes. 'I feel it's good for my mental well-being,' she smiled.

'In what way?'

'When you are serving tea, you're totally focused in the moment. There are no distractions. The ritual of serving, every step of the process, every movement, is calming and freeing. You forget all your everyday worries.'

'How long will it take you to master the tea ceremony, do you think?' I asked.

'Oh, I don't know. I think it might take me my whole life!' Naoko laughed.

Masters of the tea ceremony, I'd read, need around ten years to perfect the ceremony, but I guessed, as Naoko had suggested, a whole lifetime of practise to maintain the level of dedication and service.

My tea server bowed again, lowered herself onto her knees and with two hands took my cup from me. I was not used to being received with such graciousness. Every one of her ritualised movements had drawn me into the ceremony, and for a time, the outside world had ceased to exist.

When the women said goodbye and left, I remembered the garden outside the picture window. Autumn was at its most glorious, a riot of colour on this bright day, but mentally the Japanese were already preparing for winter. The sweet I had been given with the *matcha* tea had shown me that.

That evening, we were invited to In Kanazawa House, an old *Machiya* – a long, narrow merchant house filled with creaking wood. Two geisha girls entertained us with an evening of *sake* and music, making sure our glasses were kept full. I watched their performance as I ate from a lacquered 'lunchbox', its little compartments elegantly filled with fish, fruit and vegetables, each compartment a work of edible art.

The girls started the evening singing a song about the seasons. It wasn't a surprise; the Japanese love of nature and depiction of all four seasons was coming up frequently on my trip. It's found in *Shiki* – the painting of the four seasons side by side. It's a recurring theme in all art forms from earthenware to folding screens and handscrolls – just like the four painted wooden dolls my Japanese pen pal had sent me decades earlier. I understood her gift better now, each season equal – the harmony and balance of nature, separate, yet complementary and interdependent.

* * *

We left Kanazawa behind and travelled to the sea. On Noto Island, Hajime was waiting for us with a row of aqua green and turquoise bicycles, ready to ride with us around its north-east shore. The island lies north of Kanazawa, caught in the embrace of Nanao Bay. Here, forested hills drop down to coastal strips of bamboo groves and rice fields, where sunshine yellow contrasts bays of sea blue glass.

We set off towards the coast on our bikes, Hajime stopping to slide back the great doors of a festival store crammed with floats. He showed us a picture of the end of summer festival, a raised tree trunk soaring into the sky with a skirt of branches and twigs.

'We cut down branches into the forest so that light can reach the mushrooms. When we set the tree trunk and the cut branches on fire, it's quite a spectacle.'

Hajime and his wife, both ecologists, had moved away from city life with their children in search of a quieter existence, somewhere they could be close to nature. They had found the perfect combination of *satoyama* and *satoumi* on the island. *Sato* means settlement, *yama* means hill or mountain. *Satoumi* refers to coastal settlements, where people make a living from the sea. On Noto Island, most people look both to the hills and to the ocean for subsistence. Hajime made a living from fishing, foraging, producing local sake wine and taking tourists and school children on ecological and cultural tours, on foot or by bike.

'You need more than one job to survive here,' Hajime explained as we cycled side by side, 'and we have to support each other in the community.' Here was *wa* again, a constant presence on Noto. I wondered if it had been different in the city. I imagined a lonelier existence, life more compartmentalised.

The sense of being out of kilter on this road trip continued to overwhelm me as the week ended. I was still on an emotional high or in a deep trough of anxiety. But on that slow cycle along the coast, as in the tearoom, I felt stillness and joy. Our way followed the curves of the sea. I leaned into its Wedgewood blue and chatted with Hajime about his life on the island. Across from the yellowing rice plants, the blue of sky reflected in the waters of the paddy field, a pale rock rose vertically from the Sea of Japan with a crown of trees like hair on a head. On the lawn of Dolphin's Smile café, a man was painting the scene on a large canvas, but otherwise the coastal road lay empty in front of us. We cycled past wood-latticed seafront houses with their little plots of winter vegetables, and once a perfect grid of fish hung out to dry, eight by four.

At the end of our cycle, Hajime led us into the dim light of an old salt-making hut, then fed us hot juice on the sea's edge, its fruit gathered with his son from a wild plum tree up on the coastal forest. Hajime took a long pole and poked it under the rocks by the quay.

'I'm trying to flush out an octopus,' he said with his sweet smile, but the octopus was out of reach. We handed our bikes back as the pale light of dusk bled into watery rice fields. The early winter light felt cold, but I was warmed through with the plum juice and cycle, and the brilliant, brilliant brightness of the island's sea and sky. Like Hajime, I was in harmony with nature. My conversations with Hajime made me ponder on my own future. Tom and I wanted to move. Like Hajime, I wanted a wilder, untamed place where I could feel closer to nature. Like Hajime, I wanted to be closer to the light-giving sea.

* * *

Our journey through Gifu and Ishikawa prefectures was coming to an end. On the last day, spent on Noto Peninsula, our hosts took us to a warehouse-styled museum filled with the paraphernalia of everyday Japanese life, decades – even centuries – old. Surrounded by boxes and jars of memories full of everyday objects stacked high on shelves, an old worn-out piano and a half-broken fishing boat took centre stage in the museum, washed up on a floor of sand.

We watched a light show in Suzu Theatre Museum as the shelved boxes eerily smoked and rattled as if coming to life – the *Tsukumogami* of everyday objects in Japanese folklore. The sea rolled over the sand, the sound of the ocean and old Noto fishing songs mingling with the sweet melody of commissioned music. Millions of years washed up on the shore: fossils, seashells, flotsam and jetsam, coming and going with the thrust of the tide and the images projected; the light in the darkness. The ocean seems eternal, yet its contents were fragile and ephemeral. I started to cry, overwhelmed by the beauty of the music and the conflicting sense of eternality and transience. Japan had been too much and not enough. I longed for the familiarity of home, but at the same time I wanted to stay. Japan had more to give me: the *wa* of every season, the beauty of its mountains and seas – seemingly ageless but under threat from man and nature – the ancient shrines and Zen gardens I had still to see. The country had offered me its philosophy of harmony and balance in all things, a respect for the fleeting beauty of our world and the circular nature of life: winter's slowing down, a burst of spring, long summer days, autumn's gift of colour and back to winter again.

Then I realised I didn't have to leave the *wa* of Japan behind. I could take it home, boxed up in my own collection of memories. I could unpack it on my own island on the other side of the world and lift it up to the light in the darkness over the long winter days ahead. I would learn to accept the transient nature of life and my fragile, fleeting existence, so precious, so broken, yet held together with gold. I would use the dark days to meet the darkest thoughts with strength and resilience, if I could.

December

Putin's War

In the midst of darkness, light persists.
– Mahatma Gandhi

The previous winter, I'd watched a news report on Ukraine,
A diagram showed Putin's tanks lined up on the border of
the country like toy symbols on a Risk board. It felt unreal.
It felt far away. It felt like someone else's threat, not mine,
but I found it disturbing all the same. Putin, the newsreader
reported, promised it was a military exercise; he was not
going to invade Ukraine. Footage showed Ukrainians stroll-
ing through parks looking relaxed. Early in the morning of
the next day – on the 24th of February – the first bombs fell,
and the tanks rolled in.

Now, the long stretch of Russia had reached into our
home almost three-quarters of a year later. Energy prices
had gone through the roof – as our heating seemed to
do in our draughty house. We'd set the thermostat to 10
degrees on returning from France. I made hot water bottles
and worked beneath the warmth of a blanket. But when
December set in, the temperature plunged below zero. We
turned the thermostat up again and worried about the constant 'over budget' red on our smart meter. I lit the wood
burner and huddled over the fire. When we went out walking, we kept warm, and could turn the thermostat down for

a while. It was a constant balancing act, keeping our energy bills down and not freezing. I was glad of the hill climbs that warmed us up.

When the snow arrived on the higher ground, we drove to Hathersage and parked beneath the church. We dropped into the valley on the other side of St Michael the Archangel, coming to a wooden door framed by a single layer of stone. It led into a woodland. I hoped to find Narnia winter but instead we found autumn, a carpet of orange leaves silvered by frost. We climbed to the snowline and set off up a field, loving its pureness beneath a cloudless sky. Everything throbbed with crisp cold. We trudged up a lane lacquered with black ice and onto Stanage Edge lying under a deep layer of snow. The escarpment was busy with walkers and climbers. A man marched past in shorts.

'You're brave! Don't you feel the cold?' I shouted over to him.

'Can't afford long trousers,' he laughed.

Everyone chatted to us as we passed. It was always the way with snow – it brought out the extrovert in an otherwise reserved nation.

'I've fallen several times in the snow.' A woman giggled. 'But I love it.'

'Well, at least it's a soft landing,' I laughed. I slipped too as I picked my way down through the icy rocks of the escarpment. I didn't care. The cold was a curse but also a benediction. Walks like these would keep me going for days.

Olga's War

*Toutes les ténèbres du monde ne peuvent éteindre la lumière
d'une seule bougie. (All the darkness in the world cannot
extinguish the light of a single candle.)*
– St Francis of Assisi

There were two things that continued to carry me through
the winter: walks in nature and friendship. Olga came into my
life not long after Putin entered hers. She was keen to take
up the offer of English conversation I'd made in an online
group chat to Ukrainians hoping to settle in our small town.
Olga sent me pictures from Turkey, where she'd made her
escape from Ukraine. I opened images of turquoise coasts
and the burning rocks of Yantaras on my phone, Olga and
her family grinning at the camera as if they were on holiday.
But Turkey, once a holiday destination for Olga, was now a
temporary place of exile. The family hoped to move on to
West Europe, initially thinking of Germany before they were
offered a small flat in the Midlands of England – a place
they'd never heard or thought of. It was a far cry from the
bustling city of Kyiv where Olga had lived for many years.

Olga and I communicated regularly online while she waited
for her visa. Once in England, she told me bits and pieces of
her story: the family's harrowing escape from Kyiv, the journey
into Turkey, the sudden and unexpected invitation to England. Olga was 'lucky' in comparison to other Ukrainians – if
losing your home, a well-paid job, friends and indeed an entire
life is in any way lucky. The first stroke of good fortune was
having three children; it meant her husband, Pasha, could leave
Ukraine with her. The second was the offer of an entire flat

– their own space! Olga wasn't just lucky, though; she was energetic, pro-active and full of get up and go. She took everything life threw at her and ran with it. She came to see me the day after she arrived in town, armed with cherry dumplings. Olga immersed herself in British culture. She said yes to everything: walks in the Peak countryside; our geeky record club and film nights; summer gatherings under the stars with friends. Before long, she'd found a job with the Youth Hostel Association. Olga projected *joie de vivre*, but there was, unsurprisingly, pain she mainly kept to herself.

Olga's escape from Ukraine came out slowly: a detail here, a few details there. I started to feel ashamed. My grumbles about our rising energy bills were insignificant in comparison; Tom and I managed. My struggles with winter seemed pathetic too in comparison to what Olga had endured with the arrival of war. After the invasion – the so-called special operation – Olga didn't know if she would survive. Now, she was safe, if unanchored in a foreign county. But those left behind in Ukraine, who didn't have the money or health to walk away, were dealing with freezing winter days, sometimes without water and heating, not knowing when the Russians would send their missiles.

One evening, I invited Olga round for apple crumble. I wanted to hear her story in its entirety.

We sat around the dining room table, warmed by fruit and spice. I asked Olga what she thought about our British weather.

'Well, Helen, you've got two seasons: almost summer and almost winter.'

I laughed. Olga was right. It was rarely hot and hardly ever properly cold.

'What's winter like in Ukraine?' I asked curiously.

'Snow starts in November, when it comes and goes. In December, it freezes hard and stays on the ground, then the snow stays with us until spring.'

I thought of the winter I'd spent in the Swiss Engadine: proper winter, not 'almost winter'.

'It's not like here,' she added. 'We wear proper winter clothes – sunglasses against the bright light, warm boots and thick down coats.'

It was clear that Olga loved winter in Ukraine. But winter meant something else now: winter was war; winter was power cuts and sirens; winter was the sudden unexpected bombing of Kyiv; winter was fear of losing someone you loved. Winter was sometimes a feeling of betrayal from family and friends. Winter was a people physically, sometimes ideologically or politically, divided.

In the December before the war, a British journalist asked Olga (Chief Accountant for three apartment blocks, and one of the people involved in managing them), what they would do if there was war in Ukraine. The journalist asked to see one of the basements in Olga's remit, and noted there was no water supply, toilet facilities, only one access point and no generator if the electricity failed.

'Do you really believe the Russians would bomb us?' Olga asked.

'Of course,' the journalist replied.

Olga was unconvinced; Russians and Ukrainians had a common history and heritage. Pasha, her husband, was part Russian, as were some other Ukrainians.

Then it happened. Wednesday the 23rd of February 2022 was another ordinary day in Ukraine. Olga's middle son was preparing a gift for Woman's Day in his Design and Technology lesson. Vera, Olga's mum, was with the family, helping to prepare a welcome party for the family's new apartment.

At five o'clock the next morning, Vera woke Olga.

'The war has started,' she said.

Their life as they knew it was over.

By the end of the week, Russian soldiers had parachuted into Kyiv. At first, Olga and Pasha decided to sit it out. Unlike others in their apartment block, they had no friends or relatives they could live with in the relative safety of western Ukraine. Slowly, their apartment block emptied out until there were only a few families left. Ever practical, Olga got on with organising food and water supplies to checkpoints. The bombings intensified. The family taped up the windows, squeezing into the narrow corridor at night where there were no windows.

'How did you feel?' I asked Olga. 'It must have been petrifying.'

'It felt unreal, like watching a film of someone else's life.'

The apartment block across the green from them was bombed, disappearing into a cloud of dust. They moved out into the communal hallway with sleeping bags and camping mats, where there was no heating. Olga barely managed four hours of sleep at night, constantly waking up to scroll through her mobile for news of the war. *Were they still safe?*

Shops emptied of food along with basics like bread, and the bombings intensified. Olga and Pasha realised they had to go. They borrowed a car and drove out of the city, not knowing which, if any, petrol stations on their route would still have fuel. What if they ran out along the way?

A military acquaintance advised them on a safe route to Smila. From Smila, the journey was fraught with road checks, their documents checked and rechecked. Progress was slow. They stayed with friends in Vinnytsia for a night, all but out of petrol. But the journey to Lviv was becoming impossible. The plan to meet her brother, who was to take her mother on to his house, was ditched: he believed it now too dangerous to leave the safety of his home. And indeed, Vinnytsia was bombed the day after Olga and her family departed. Instead of driving further west, they headed south to Mohyliv-Podil's'kyi.

It had taken them five days to reach the border with Moldova, a journey that would have taken a fraction of the time before the war. As they drove west, Olga's hands shook, afraid they would be ambushed on the way; afraid for their lives.

'I still have nightmares about the journey,' Olga said quietly.

They crossed over Moldova into Romania, both countries offering them food and shelter before they continued to Turkey. War brings out the best and worst in humans. Life is filled with darkness and light, figuratively and literally. Inhumanity sits side by side with extraordinary acts of kindness. Ukrainians were now living a life of uncertainty with no idea what the future would hold; not only those in Ukraine, but also those who found themselves washed up on foreign shores. And yet, Olga carried on with good humour and positivity. It was a privilege to know her. While she was metaphorically wintering on someone else's island, waiting out the darkness of war so she could return home, paradoxically, she was a light in my winter anxiety.

Christmas with a Ukrainian Family

Car c'est en donnant qu'on reçoit. (For it is in giving that we receive.)
– St Francis of Assisi

Three generations came: Olga's mum, Vera, and her newly arrived husband, Vlad (with no English but an easy smile), Olga, Pasha and their three sons, Vanya, Illia and Vadym. My own sons were also home. Tom and I were in a flap cooking for eleven. There were normally only four of us, and we wanted our Ukrainian family to enjoy our traditional food. We extended our table as far as we could, but it was still not big enough, so we squeezed our campervan table onto the end.

Olga, curious about our British Christmas, had been delighted to accept our invitation. The Orthodox traditions around Christmas and New Year in Ukraine followed the Gregorian calendar, starting on Christmas Eve – the 6th of January – and finishing on the 19th of January with the Baptism of Christ celebration. On Sviat Vechir – Holy Evening on the 6th of January, Orthodox Ukrainians prepare twelve dishes, each representing the twelve apostles. According to tradition, you shouldn't begin to eat until the first star appears in the sky, marking the birth of Jesus. The abundance of dishes called *Bohata Vecherya* – Rich Dinner – included *kutia* (wheat, barley or rice), *uzvar* (a fruit drink), vinaigrette, a potato and vegetable salad, *vareniki* (dumplings), cabbage soup, pickles, borscht, buckwheat, stuffed cabbages, vegetable stew, patties and baked apples. How could we compete? We bought a large turkey, then thinking it inadequate, added a brute-sized ham – enough to feed a Ukrainian army, not two families. We prepared a Christmas broth, Brussel sprouts, carrots, roast parsnips and potatoes along with stuffing and pigs in blankets. For dessert, we offered trifle and Christmas pudding. We hoped we had done the British Christmas justice.

There is something cheering about sharing food. Christmas meals with friends and family were easing me through the darkest days. No wonder the unknown birth date of Christ had been plucked from December and January. And there was also something especially poignant about sharing a meal with a family displaced. But this was a joyous gathering, an exchange of silliness and fellowship with the King's speech (a royal tradition Tom and I had long abandoned), games and an exchange of gifts.

Olga handed me a framed embroidered picture, a heart with the word *love* woven into its centre. If it had been on a Christmas card, it would have felt twee, but I thought of Olga in her busy life stitching my gift night on night. Love isn't a word that comes easy to me, brought up in the emotionally austerity of a Scots-Presbyterian culture in Northern Ireland, but there is nothing more crucial to the human condition.

I had wanted to give the arriving Ukrainians a welcome to ease their passage into our foreign country: English lessons, friendship and a shared experience of our culture, but it felt like I was receiving far more in return. Not just Vera's *vareniki*, Pasha's pancakes and Olga's offerings of Ukrainian sweet nibbles (she never arrived at my house empty-handed), but the family's openness of heart in the dampness of our winter, in the coldness of Putin's war.

January

New Year Heights

Nature always wears the colors of the spirit.
– Ralph Waldo Emerson

'Let's climb Masson Hill to greet in the dawning of the new year,' Patrick said.

He knocked on my bedroom door with a cup of tea in the predawn. I slowly came to, sluggish from our New Year celebrations that had continued well after midnight. Quietly, I cursed Patrick.

Still, I flung on clothes in the icy darkness of my bedroom. Soon, we were dropping down into town; cracks of yellowy light appeared in the sky. Would we beat the sunrise? We spoke in low voices, enjoying the quietness of the early morning, glad to be in each other's company. Mother and son, past the stormy years, settling into a mutual respect. As we climbed the sledging field, we paused to look back at our town with its giant crane – Lifty McShifty – shoring up the River Derwent that had taken away parts of buildings in some of the country's worst floods. The crane rose above the town, bright with its Christmas decorations, set among the scattering of quiet streets with the first glows of window lights on the Bank, early risers getting dressed. We reached the track near the top of Masson Hill, where we'd eaten chocolate and coffee during the pandemic, when our views had extended our world far beyond the few miles we'd been granted in lockdown. The sky was now spreading pale pink and yellow, the sun just edging the trees above the horizon.

'Look, Patrick, the sun,' I said as I panned round with my phone camera, the orange quarter on the horizon a halo above his head.

'Which son?' he laughed with typical Patrick corny humour.

We climbed higher, trying to find the summit. We reached a high point. Was it here? We weren't sure, but it didn't matter. The world was ours, spread out below our feet, the sky a flare of New Year light. We headed down the copse where we'd found the spiral of daffodils at the beginning of lockdown, and stood in a corner, sheltering from the wind to drink water and eat shortbread – a strange New Year break-fast. In the lockdowns, the swirl of daffodils had felt like a symbol of hope. I thought of the Japanese celebration of the transitional nature of life, their love for the fleeting beauty of the cherry blossom, their acceptance of life and death, even the brutal changes brought about by nature. The lockdowns already seemed a distant memory. Nothing remains static: the hurtling circle of the seasons showed us that year on year.

Heading down Salters Lane, there was no sign of the buzzards' calls, just our chatter filling the air. Back in the house, we ate a second breakfast with my visiting sister and her husband. This was the way to start the year, with buttery toast and steaming coffee.

I thought of the countless Japanese festivals paying homage to the seasons. I would mark the dark of the new year, the achingly slow lengthening of days, with friendships and celebrations, I promised myself, and long rambles in nature's healing.

Winter Winds

Come Faeries, take me out of this dull world,
for I would ride with you upon the wind and dance upon the
mountains like a flame!
– William Butler Yeats

I was in the search of our most ancient worlds high on the Peak. The day was grey, the sky in constant flux, daggers of light falling on trees on the distant horizon. I marched along the High Peak Trail, a dismantled railway, Minninglow in front of me, beckoning me on. This clump of trees can be seen from miles away across the White Peak, its distinctive circle of outer and inner trees easily identifiable among the many thickets that sit on the skyline. From the air, the perfect circle of trees with its taller beeches at its centre looks like a winter garland.

I headed past a disused quarry, a rusting crane in front of it. A little further on, a fingerpost pointed the way to Minninglow. I weaved my way through wary sheep and on through a gate into the embrace of the wooded enclosure. There was a stillness in this ancient place where Neolithic and Bronze Age man, as well as Romans, had left their mark. The site is strewn with ancient tomb stones and two Bronze Age barrows. I sat on one of the flat limestone capstones of a burial chamber and drank my coffee, the trees barely a whisper, the wind held back. This was a place of the dead: human bones had been found here. But it was also a place of the active living: Roman bronzes, coins and pottery had been excavated along with flint knives, a bronze razor and bone tool. I wondered if I was being disrespectful, sitting on the capstone of a burial chamber. I imagined not. It felt like I was sitting in conversation with my early Neolithic ancestors.

Well, how was it back then? Was it hard? Do you envy us with all our creature comforts, or do you think we've lost our way? I'm not sure I'd have coped with your existence – always close to death, living life on the edge. But yes, it's true; we've lost something you had. Did your animal wildness make you feel more alive? I bet it did. Our world is sterilised; we've cut ourselves off from the nature we share the planet with. We've on some level disconnected from Earth, even though we're living on it. We think nothing of trashing the only home we have. We've built walls of brick and stone and metal as we move from house to car and car to house. We've forgotten our place in the solar system. Where's the Milky Way, you ask? We drowned it out with our artificial lights. Yes, I concur: we barely see the stars with all the man-made light we've created. The moon doesn't guide us – we use the torches on our phones, and that's if we go out in the darkness at all. It's true, we don't know what it's like to fight for survival. We no longer experience the deep satisfaction of a meal after long hours of hunting. Everything's physically easy, but mentally hard. Would I join you if I could go back in time? Experience that primitive wildness? I wouldn't have the courage. I'm too soft. Yes, it's been nice talking to you too. You've been lovely ghosts.

In reality, of course, all I had was my imagination. I knew little of how my early ancestors had lived and what they felt about their existence. Still, sitting there with my sandwiches among my friendly ghosts, I recognised they had something modern man had lost somewhere along the way: a close connection with nature. Beyond the trees of the burial site, the land had become a wildlife desert of upland fields – not much good for hunting or wildlife. How would I explain to my ancient ancestors we had lost half of our biodiversity in the UK? I wondered if there were trees surrounding the burial chambers back then, or had man already started to decimate our flora and fauna? The highest areas were the first to be cleared in Neolithic times, when hunter-gatherers were transitioning to farming. I knew so little about these forefathers – only the physical evidence of their unscripted lives. Had they buried those excavated tools with the dead? They had grown crops and kept livestock but still hunted for deer and gathered berries. I imagined, like the Arctic Finns, they were in tune with nature, while focused on self-preservation. Like the Japanese, they would have worked in harmony with the turning of the seasons, storing up food for the lean times of winter, hunkering down in their caves or simple dwellings when darkness fell, working together against the elements. I imagined their acceptance of their tough existence. What else could they do?

I sat quietly for a while longer among the burial stones, unperturbed by the dead. The day was ragged, damp and chilled, but I felt at peace in the shelter of the beeches among the stones. Eventually, I stirred and clambered down the other side of the hill. I marched stony High Peak farm tracks, racing the daylight. The wind was whipping up, slamming my face. Clouds formed and reformed, changing colour from pale primrose to rose. I met no one on the second straight-as-a-die track of rubble. No man or dog was mad enough to leave the shelter of home, just me. But there was something pleasing about being alone in this upland landscape, the wind numbing my cheekbones, the dusk fast approaching. I felt no fear. I only had the land for company, the crunch of stone beneath my feet, the sweep of field and drystone wall and the arch of sky. I felt at ease in this place. It was almost dark when I reached the car. I switched on the engine for warmth, drank the rest of my coffee and made for home.

The long march and the winter winds had woken me out of my lethargy, my prehistoric ancestors reminding me of my place in the natural world. I wrote in my gratitude diary: *my nature-wise Stone Age ancestors; the energy of the wind; being alone but not lonely.*

Searching for Ancestors

As on this whirligig of Time, We circle with the seasons
– Alfred, Lord Tennyson

Olga and Pasha looked at our snow boots in surprise.

'They're warm and waterproof,' I explained. Pasha and Olga had not yet encountered our winter mud. It had rained so long the fields and woodlands were a quagmire. Our Ukrainian friends were wearing lightweight walking boots, spotlessly clean, unlike mine and Tom's, covered in caked mud.

As we climbed down towards the hermit's cave, slipping and sliding through trees, Olga told me friends back home had been playing hockey on a frozen lake. Life was going on as normal between the bombs.

Having paid homage to my medieval hermit, we crossed to Robin Hood's Stride and clambered to its top. The White and Dark Peak spread out in all the directions. To the north, the remaining four stones of Nine Stone Close huddled together in an intimate circle – the tractor now gone. We too huddled together in our human circle, warming up with hot drinks from our flasks. The sun's rays were weak on our faces, but after endless days of grey, the powder blue skies were a relief.

The stone circle of Nine Stones Close sits in a private field, some distance from the public footpath, but the open gate seemed to invite trespass. We plodded through clag to reach the stone circle, Olga not at all impressed with the mud but curious to see the prehistoric monument up close. Bronze Age flints and potsherds had been excavated here. Several stones had been carted off and repurposed in an act of vandalism – one used as a gatepost. I wondered who had taken them. Farmers, probably. Hadn't they known what the stones were? Or had they not cared?

We dropped down a field below the Castle Ring, an ancient defence settlement with an earthwork ditch, prehistoric activity in evidence all over Harthill Moor. At the bottom of the field, we forded the stream, the farmland on the other side saturated with water. My boots were covered in mud, even my trousers from crossing mud-splattered stiles. Olga, magically, inexplicably, had mud-free boots and hardly a mark on her light-coloured leggings.

'Did you fly?' I teased Olga. 'Are you a white witch?'

Olga teased me back with jabs about our 'almost winter'.

We abandoned the fields and stuck to the roads, flying down Dudwood Lane, Robin Hood's Stride fading out in the dusk.

* * *

Two days later, Tom and I were back on the hunt of Derbyshire's high-level Neolithic and Bronze Age monuments. The temperature had suddenly dropped, and snow had finally arrived after weeks of rain. With the strong sun, however, it had already melted on south-facing fields. We were walking through landscapes of green and white.

On Derby Lane, we stepped aside as a tractor approached. The farmer stopped and warned us to be careful on the icy lane.

'Treacherous,' he said, holding up a hot water bottle. I looked at it in surprise.

'I'm taking it to the cattle. The water trough is covered in a thick layer of ice. I need to melt it with the hot water. Unfortunately, I've got to keep these cattle outside because I have another herd in the byre for now.' He shook his head. 'They're eating twice as much outside with the cold snap.'

When we caught up with him, he was striding across the field, the hot water bottle in one hand, a spade in the other. I watched him drop down to the trough in the corner of the field, slamming the ice with his spade before throwing hot water into the icy liquid.

The elderly farmer had a toughness to him from living in the outdoors. I imagined he didn't dwell much on winter anxiety. He'd have experienced many a bleak winter on the Peak uplands. He'd have dealt with winter year on year in a no-nonsense, practical way – finding solutions, caring for his animals through wind, snow and rain. I could learn from his resilience.

We continued up the lane, the sun warming my back, the glints of ice in the snow a dazzle, the sky filled with bright, bright light. I felt my back straighten and my mood soar. The light! The bright snow! Olga would have called the patchwork of green and white surrounding us almost winter too, but this was good enough for me. It was more than good enough. It was pure joy.

Ahead, flooding in the lane's dip had frozen hard. Tom and I slammed stones onto the ice, trying to break its surface. Now and again, the water bubbled up with a plop on impact, but mostly the stones just skidded across the ice. We laughed at our efforts, the snow and ice bringing out our inner children.

We rounded a corner and saw a fox. I watched him leap effortlessly over a drystone wall; lean, muscled, strong. A young male, probably. He was a beautiful creature, fiery red with a thick bushy tail. The fox started up the field on the other side of the boundary, then froze, catching sight of Tom and me.

These were the winter moments that sustained me, those unexpected glimpses into the natural world. The sight of the fox drew me into his world, caught me up in the here and now, returned me to my place in the Earth, a part of its whole. The dog and I eye-balled each other for a few seconds, then he was off, bounding up the field, orange-bright against the snow, before disappearing. I tried to imagine the fox's life, most of it spent in search of food. How difficult was it in the snow? I imagined wildlife would have gone underground, although Tom had spotted rabbit tracks. There would be plenty of rodents and carrion to feed on. The fox had sensed me from a long way off. He would easily sniff out rabbits and mice, even under a covering of snow. Later, I read foxes have an athletic pounce, rearing up and landing on front paws with enough force to smash through a thick crust of snow.

At Upper Oldhams Farm, we climbed up to Arbor Low, appearing as a snowy hill on the skyline. We reached its henge – a wide bank and ditch, enfolding a Neolithic circle of great slabs of stone. Unlike other Peak stone circles, the stones were all lying on the ground. Medieval Christians had perhaps pushed them over, fearing the pagan site. It was an act of vandalism to match the Harthill Moor farmers. Tom and I circled the henge, the higher hummock at one end a Bronze Age burial mound. Beneath the tumulus, cremated and interred human bones, flints, pottery and an antler had been excavated, a physical story of an unrecorded life.

Here, the hills of the White Peak plateau on the horizon were a perfect echo of the henge, a 360-degree circle of sky and upland. Early Neolithic man had sought out this high place where heaven and earth come together. The high-level stone circles are the prehistoric equivalent of the church spires that would come later; man wanting to get as close to God as possible, or to the otherworld. And on this high plateau, I too felt my spirit soar. At this prehistoric site, where ceremonial activity extends back between 3,000 and 6,000 years, Neolithic and Bronze Age peoples were close to nature and the turning of the seasons. They were closely bound with the rhythms of the land, like my ghosts on Minninglow, and would have accepted winter's part in the four seasons. Life was brutal and short, but they would have lived in the moment, focused on finding food like the fox.

And in this world where hills and sky enfolded me - winter anxiety felt far away.

Leaving the nearby Gib Hill burial barrow, Tom and I tumbled down to the farm and on through fields to a tangled Cales Dale, an obstacle course of frosted stalks and fallen trees, hemmed in by rocky cliffs where pointed icicles hung from overhangs. At the junction of Lathkill Dale, the sheer limestone walls of the valley in front of us were bathed in incandescent light, orange-bright like the fox's back. We climbed up through the dale, the river coursing downhill with such a force it was difficult to believe it would dry up in summer. We came to its source, gushing from the mouth of a cave where it had emerged from underground streams.

The light was ebbing away as we tramped back into Monyash, but I no longer feared the dusk and the approaching night on our walks. January, always the toughest of months, had not been that bad – in fact, it felt fine, and now, more than halfway through, winter was edging towards spring, dark yielding to light in the circle of life. I knew that, just as prehistoric man did.

Rabbie Burns

Fair fa' your honest sonsie face
Great Chieftain o' the Puddin-race!
– Robert Burns

'So, you know what haggis is?' I asked Olga and Pasha. They smiled and waited.

'It's a bird that lives on the Scottish hills,' I said solemnly, 'one leg longer than the other, so they can only go round the mountain clockwise. The hunters lie in wait at the bottom of the mountain, making a noise to frighten the haggis. Confused, they start to run around the hill in the wrong direction, then tumble off the slope – and straight into the nets of the hunters.'

Olga and Pasha laughed: they were nobody's fool.

We'd invited our Ukrainian friends to experience another

British tradition – this one from across the border. We decided to combine Burns Night celebrations with our nerdy Record Club. In our kitchen, the table was laid out with food and drink. Outside, a smattering of snow lay on the ground. Inside, the kitchen was warm from the oven and the bodies of friends huddled together with drinks, ready to toast the laird. Tom was kitted out in his kilt, sporran and *Sgian Dubh* – knife – tucked into a thick woollen sock.

Standing ceremoniously in front of the haggis, he began his poem.

> *His knife see Rustic-labour dight*
> *An' cut you up wi' ready slight*

Tom lifted a sharp knife high above his head and brought it down hard on the haggis, piercing the lining of sheep stomach.

> *Trenching your gushing entrails bright*
> *Like onie ditch.*

He sliced through the haggis.

> *And then what a glorious sight,*
> *Warm, reeking, rich!*

The stomach lining split, and heart, liver and lungs spewed across the plate, the ingredients bound together with sheep's lard and oats and spiced with pepper.

There was much gesticulation as Tom recited the poem, seeking to provide visual clues for our guests, who could only

otherwise cling to the standard English words and phrases
sprinkled through the dialect.

Clap in his walie nieve a blade,
He'll mak it whissle;
An' legs, an' arms, an' heads will sned,
like taps o'thristle.

Tom took the knife again and brandished it through the
air, back and forth. Our guests gave a nervous laugh and
leaned away from the mad Scotsman.

Auld Scotland wants nae skinking ware,
That jaups in luggies;
But if ye wish her gratefu' prayer,
Gie her a haggis!

He finished with a flourish. Raising his glass of whisky,
Tom knocked some back and drenched the haggis with the
rest.

Fortunately for the Scots, Rabbie Burns was born in
one of the coldest, darkest months of winter – on the 25th
of January 1759. It's a convenient time to celebrate the
birth of their national poet, when sunset arrives hot – or
cold – on the heels of sunrise. It enables them to break up
the depressing months of grey and dark with dancing and
song, food and whisky. With a Scottish husband, I celebrate Burns Night every year. It's no wonder the tradition
is creeping into English pubs south of the border, the long
months between New Year and Easter otherwise barren of
festivities.

That evening with our Record Club group, we listened to Scottish music and finished with a spirits-fuelled sing-along. *Donald, Where's Your Troosers?* is more fun when you've had a belly full of Scottish malt whisky. Our night had brought laughter and joviality into the dullness of a dreary January.

I've always wondered why England, my adopted country, hasn't created a nationwide festival to break up those quiet months after the new year like the Scots and mainland Europeans. Across the Continent, villages, towns and cities celebrate Carnival before Lent around Shrove Monday and Tuesday – a time of fasting, or at least sacrifice. In England, we may mark Shrove Tuesday with pancakes, but it's hardly party time. In contrast, the carnival floats and parades of mainland Europe bring singing and dancing, outrageous outfits, accompanied by food and copious amounts of drink. Over the years, I've witnessed the excitement of *Fasnacht* in Zurich, the political satire floats of Maastricht and the oom-pah bands of Cologne. In the snowy February of 1994, I took part in Blankenheim's *Geisterzug* – the ghost parade – in the heart of the Eifel in North Rhine-Westphalia. Blankenheim's winter carnival reminds us that Christian festivals supersede Pagan rituals. The *Geisterzug* is still rooted in Pagan times. Blankenheim's townspeople dress up in white bed-sheets, creating ears with elastic bands, before covering their faces in powder. They are the spring – and springing ghosts – banishing winter spirits and heralding in the season of new growth with their Blankenheim festive song and dance. It's a bizarre sight, the town full of spirit-like figures, faces ghoul-ish in the light of their firebrands as they take to the medieval streets with their strange hopping dance.

In Japan, winter festivals celebrating the light in the darkness are found across all its islands. From the Sapporo Snow Festival, Lake Shikotsu Ice Festival, Sounkyo Ice-fall Festival and Otaru Snow Light Path Festival on the northern island of Kokkaido to the Night Festival of Chichibu on Honshu and Nagasaki Lantern Festival on the southern island of Kyushu, Japan is illuminated over the winter months. More than any other time of year, we need to create light in the darkest weeks of January and February.

And in my gratitude diary, I wrote down: *friendships; laughter; celebrations.*

February

In the Blackness of Night

*And God divided the light from the darkness. And God called
the light Day, and the darkness he called Night.*
– Genesis 1:4-5

It has happened so gradually I hadn't noticed it: I'd made
peace with winter. My mind was calm. Sleep came easily. I
appreciated what daylight there was and I welcomed in the
night. I found it more difficult to accept the grey. Perhaps I
would continue to greet winter with some resistance, but now,
three years into winter reflection and mindfulness, I realised
I was making progress. Maybe it was like putting on an old
pair of winter boots again; I needed time to re-familiarise
myself. I needed time to adapt to the rationed light. I'd
drawn strength from friendships, old and new. My travel
writing had taken me from the wilds of Iceland, figuratively,
and out into the Peak District countryside, physically. I was
busy in my work and its occupation was good for me. I felt
privilege in my wanderings, inside my head, conjured up on
the page and in real time. I knew I was blessed.

February brought days to a close with dramatic skies with
colours to match November's autumn show. I watched our
valley deepen in colour from grey to charcoal to smoked pink
and blood red; mackerel skies. I watched clouds ripple out like
tidal waves, as if flowing in and around coral reefs. I didn't
mind the black curtain fall of the day's end. I stopped dreading

putting out the light for fear of where my mind would take me. Beyond the brighter days of winter, precious friendships, the nourishment of food and soul and the healing of nature, I was learning to deal with feelings of abandonment, rejection and judgement. I had stumbled on a country singer called Travis Meadows – goodness knows how, as country music was not a musical genre I enjoyed. But the lyrics of his song *Sideways* hit me with the force of a truck, the chorus refrain repeating the words *push it down and it comes out sideways*. I had done so much pushing down over the last years. It had been my way of coping. In the darkness of the night, I realised I could no longer push down on those feelings that weighed me down like a stone. They were coming out sideways. I sat in conversation with myself. I realised in the darkest hours, I was not the author of anyone else's thoughts and beliefs, and neither had I any entitlement to them – only my own. I acknowledged my hurt. I tried to understand the pain I had unintentionally caused others, the hurt we cause each other because we are reading from different scripts. I learned acceptance. I learned not to reflect on the weaknesses of others because they reflected back at me. Those who had damaged me also felt fear and anger and hurt as I did. They too felt vulnerable in a world of contradictions. They too were trying to make sense of an imperfect world. I needed to focus, not on human weaknesses of ego and pride, but instead on human kindness – on love, which had been demonstrated down through the years to me in so many small and bigger ways. All those little acts of kindness had informed me as a person. It was so easy to forget all that in the storms of adult life. All of us were muddling along, imperfectly. Those lessons were hard to learn, but learn them I had to. The darkness of winter had taught me that.

I had reflected and grown. Occasionally, I would backslide. I would acknowledge my own judgement, my own anger and bitterness. I would acknowledge a sense of deep betrayal, then move on, because I knew others felt betrayed by me too. Bitter thoughts had poisoned me and I'd become a victim to my own dark thoughts. I knew I would have to relearn the lessons again and again, just as I had to relearn a love of winter. But each time, it would be easier – quicker.

The darkness of night, with no other distractions, helped me combat my gremlins, problem solve and think creatively. I had my best ideas lying in bed in the blackness, no other stimulation getting in the way of my thought processes. I stopped worrying if sleep was slow to come: the night fed my imagination. At the same time, I had more control over my ability to fall asleep. The repeated words of learned poetry – like a comfort blanket – emptied my mind of all thoughts, carrying me into oblivion. Sleep, like winter, is restorative. Darkness produces melatonin. It makes us groggy and sleepy and suppresses brain activity, a bit like a dimmer switch. When sleep arrives, it repairs our brains as well as our bodies. In the sleep-inducing darkness, our brains process information and consolidate memory. In deep sleep, blood pressure drops, and our heart rate slows, giving our bodies a well-earned rest from the endless daytime activity. Our bodies are naturally in tune with the divisions of day and night. We are programmed to sleep at night. And in the longer darker hours of winter, we slow down and sleep even more. Winter sluggishness is beneficial to our health, just as it's restorative in plants, trees and animals.

Now, when I switched off the light, I welcomed in the black. When I closed my eyes, sealing in the darkness, it was a joy to float off into unconsciousness – to fall away from the endless flow of thoughts. In Kathleen Jamie's book *Findings,* she challenges the negative connotations of darkness – the centuries-old Christian metaphor for wrongdoing and evil. Yet in the story of the Creation, God divides day from night. One follows the other. They're given equal weight, just as the Japanese give the four seasons equal weight. As the Earth rotates away from the sun, it casts the shadow of night. It's a natural phenomenon. Day and night, summer and winter, warmth and cold, hand and glove – one cannot exist without the other, at least not in the northern hemisphere.

Kathleen Jamie reminds us that we start life in the darkness of the womb. It's a place of comfort – that recall I'd sensed in the belly of the forest in the Finnish Arctic Circle. Night takes us back to the place of our beginning. We curl up in the foetal position. Darkness envelops us. We float into sleep. It returns us to a state of unknowing, a state of innocence. In this place of unconsciousness, there is no past, there is no future. We are born again.

Winter Music

Love, love, love, that is the soul of the genius.
– Wolfgang Amadeus Mozart

Tom and I climbed through upland fields. February was inching towards March. Snowdrops and crocuses seemed to have appeared from nowhere. Daffodils were on the cusp of opening.

'Listen,' said Tom. 'The skylarks are singing again.'

'I can't hear them,' I replied with frustration in my voice.

'But they're loud and clear,' he said as he pointed to the sky above us. A pair fluttered on the air; dots high in the heavens. I stood still, watching. The presence of the skylarks told me winter was coming to an end.

We walked higher through drystone walls. At last, I heard the skylarks' music: the intricate performance of song, the rearrangements on a repertoire of notes, the sweet tunefulness and sharp clarity of voice, the buzzes and trills. It was the sound of summer and warmer weather, although the air was still cold. Other birdsong was growing in intensity too. Small birds, flying from branch to branch in leafless trees: coal tit, blue tit, chaffinch and wren. I had missed their vivacious songs over winter.

At home, after the clear skies of the skylarks, it was overcast again. I felt the deadening of my own emotions, lacking in colour, lacking in vitality, lacking in light now I was back indoors. I turned my laptop up to its highest volume, put on my headphones, closed my eyes and listened to the wall of sound from the *Introitus* of Mozart's *Requiem in D Minor*. The piece was ever present in our house as Tom practised his tenor part for an upcoming concert. I'd also sung this choral music several times over the years. Nothing moved me like this requiem. It felt sublime. It felt as if it accessed a place beyond the normal reach of humanity. It made me feel alive in the way the song of the skylark did. Mozart was gifting me the highest levels of emotional awareness.

I rarely cried. It was as if I'd deliberately switched off the tap to my deepest feelings. Was it to protect myself from hurt? I remember sitting on the empty bed where my mother had died, her body newly removed, the bed barely cold, willing myself to feel some emotion. But all I'd felt was the dullest ache of loss. Now, the tears flowed down my face. The beauty of the music touched the core of my soul. Mozart had managed to reach out to me from beyond the grave, down all those centuries, in a way no one else could.

Et lux perpetua luceat eis, the choir sang – *and let the light shine perpetually*. I had always thought Mozart's music divine, but now I realised it was the opposite: it was fully human. The movements have moments of unadulterated light and joy; they also have moments of utter darkness, fear and anguish as in the terrible beauty of the *Dies Irae* – The Day of Wrath. Light can never be *in perpetuum*. We can only appreciate it if we've experienced the surrounding darkness, and it is the light and shade of the requiem, so starkly contrasted, that makes it a work of such emotionally intensity. It's in the *Confutatis* and *Lacrimosa*, in its tenderness and brutality, its phrases of quiet and loud, in the call and response of the male and female voices – voices of judgement and plea – side by side. It's the conversation of all humanity. I lost myself in the sorrow, joy and serenity of *Agnus Dei*, the swell of strings weaving through voice conjuring up every human emotion. The tears started again. How could the spectrum of human emotion be so achingly present within a few phrases of music?

Once, I'd sung the requiem on a weekend workshop in the east of Switzerland, far from the tourist routes. We'd practised in a room with floor-to-ceiling windows, the hills on the other side of the valley a purity of snow. The absolute beauty of the music, the light and the Thurgau hills had filled me with joy and a deep peace. It had been such a privilege to sing this work in this place that winter so long ago. Mozart had lived with light and darkness all his life. He'd suffered from poor health and had written the unfinished requiem on his deathbed. He'd spent his short life acutely aware of death's closeness and had poured, paradoxically, all his being into living. His passion for life found expression in his music.

The requiem came to an end. I opened my eyes. The clouds had left an opening, revealing a circle of blue in the grey, light pouring through. The requiem, like the skylarks' song, had breathed life back into my soul.

A Japanese Garden in England

The mind is everything. What you think, you become.
– Buddha

I hadn't forgotten Japan. It was still with me. This country on the opposite side of the world had got under my skin. Of all the places I had visited in Gifu and Ishikawa prefectures, Suzu Theatre Museum on Noto Peninsula had stayed with me most: the rattling boxes; the beam of light in the darkness from the projector, spilling out an ocean floor over millennia; the harmony of nature, seemingly eternal, yet fragile and ephemeral; the haunting Japanese sea shanties and sweetly soaring orchestral music, ebbing and flowing like the ocean. Japan was far away but close. When I went out walking on grey days, I remembered the country's philosophical approach to the seasons. I saw myself more and more at one with winter, in harmony with it, as the Japanese were. I fought against its elements less and less. I wanted to go back to Japan and learn more about its philosophical culture without the debilitating anxiety I'd felt when there, but it was not possible. And it had an environmental cost. Then I remembered the Japanese Zen gardens I'd visited in early summer in an old mining village close to home. Back then, I'd taken Yuri, a newly arrived Ukrainian looking for work, to visit its owner, Alan Clements. Cascade Gardens are set in the drama of the Peak District fringes in the steep-sided dale of Bonsall, the meditation gardens caught in a long hollow below an old quarry face and an almost vertical wooded hillside. From the ruins of a cornmill next to Alan's house, a waterfall tumbles over its edge to where a waterwheel once turned, its waters fed by Bonsall Brook that cascades down through the dale and gardens. It's a place of extraordinary beauty and tranquillity, the surrounding quintessential Midlands landscape swaddling a series of sculpted gardens that look exotically Oriental.

That summer visit had taken place because Alan's Ukrainian wife was keen to support the newly arrived fellow Ukrainians in our area. She wanted to gift them a visit to Cascades, hoping they could find healing in the peace of the meditation gardens. Alan was also able to offer Yuri some work on the four acres. When we sat down at the garden table, the sun warm, the garden full of colour, the faint hum of bee in the air, I saw the stress fall away from Yuri's face and his body relax as he chatted to Alesia in Russian: at last, he'd found someone he could communicate with unhindered. Alesia and Yuri discovered they both came from the Ukrainian city of Korosten, and when Alesia found out Yuri had worked at a university horticultural department before fleeing Ukraine, they delighted in the coincidences.

As Alesia chatted to Yuri about the garden work, Alan told me his story – and how the gardens had come into existence. Decades earlier, he'd married a French woman. They'd had a son together, and soon she was pregnant again, this time with a daughter. It seemed they were creating the perfect life in their idyllic Cotswold home. But then his wife miscarried, and shortly after she was diagnosed with terminal liver cancer. When she died, Alan was devastated. What purpose did life serve? What had his wife done to deserve this fate? Why had he been made to suffer in this way? He decided, having studied the eastern religions and philosophy at university, he would try to meet the Dalai Lama. His friends laughed: meet the Dalai Lama? Everyone wants to meet the Dalai Lama! He had no chance! But six months later, he found himself invited into the home of His Holiness. The spiritual leader told him he needed to achieve complete calmness and peace of mind to find happiness again. Most of all, he needed to learn to love himself before he could love others. Meditation would help. Hope was crucial; he needed to recognise every negative event was just a temporary setback. Four years later, Alan bought Cascades House with its long narrow plot of land. After decades of neglecting the garden, Alan cleared the wilderness, planted and nourished flowers, bushes and trees, and created serene oriental gardens around his English roses. Every corner of the sheltered valley was a place to quietly meditate in – a space he wanted to share with others.

One evening, Alan sat in the garden at twilight as darkness descended, as was his habit, lost to his surroundings and removed from any internal thoughts. In this place, there was just the present. He'd become one with the nature around him. The shadowy trees on the clifftop spoke to him; the ancient yews sustained by the waters of the brook too. He tuned into the evening throb of frog and the music of the cascading waters and lost all sense of self. As the moon shone on the pale limestone cliffs, its energy reflecting back at him, he felt the calmness and peace the Dalai Lama had spoken of. All this Alan wrote down as a poem. His experience resonated. I too had felt the healing power of nature on my walks. I'd lost myself in the external world. I had forgotten myself, even in the darkness of winter, sometimes because of the darkness of winter.

But what about winter for Alan? Was he able to benefit from the garden while it lay dormant? I got in touch with Alesia and asked if I could have another chat with Alan. I wanted to know whether this time of fallow in the garden was difficult for him. Alesia sent me wintry photographs of Cascades, the garden meditation benches covered in a deep layer of snow, Alan's colourful Tibetan prayer flags bright in the monochrome landscape, the buddhas' heads crowned in white, the Japanese bridge a startling red in the black and white of brook and snow, early spring flowers buckled under the weight of the fall.

When I arrived, there was no snow, just a persistent rain that had fallen all morning. Alan made me a coffee and we settled down to chat. I asked him about his state of mind in winter outside the growing season.

'There's always something growing in the garden all year round,' he replied. 'At the moment, we have hundreds of snowdrops. The seasons are an important part of mindfulness: Buddha reminds us, every day is a new day. I still walk the garden. I know every plant in these four acres and how well each one is thriving through spring, summer, autumn and winter.'

We went outside, the garden silvered in rain, the ground saturated with water. Snowdrops lay limp in the grass. But the waterfall over the stone ruins of the old cornmill was in full flow, the curtain of water a cascade of energy on this dull day. A winter's gift.

'There are twenty benches in the garden,' Alan told me. 'Each space landscaped round the seats – wrapped in nature, bathed in nature! The benches help our visitors to get into the right frame of mind to meditate. There is a feeling of harmony and balance in these spaces, which is always at the forefront of my mind when designing the gardens.'

Harmony and balance – the Japanese approach to life I'd been so accurately aware of in Gifu and Ishikawa. After Alan's involvement with the Dalai Lama and charity work in Tibet, he discovered the monasteries and Zen gardens of Kyoto and Nara, now drawn to Japanese Zen Buddhism that focused on being at one with nature. The meditation garden designs of Cascades, I saw, were strongly influenced by Alan's visits to the Land of the Rising Sun.

In the blustery winter winds and rains, we wandered through the Japanese garden, Alan clutching his umbrella. The rain danced on the Oriental ponds where two mallards had set up home, the curved red bridge spanning the recently widened channel of water. The bright footbridge brought back to me the places I'd visited in the Japanese Alps and on the Sea of Japan.

We came to the newly created Zen Garden with its eight steps ascending to Buddha – The Noble Eightfold Path. Next to it was a gravel garden with the black and white circular symbol of Yin and Yang, opposite and complementary. I didn't need the symbolism of Buddhism or its formal teachings to appreciate its message of balance and harmony. I now understood that without the darkness, I could not appreciate the light; without winter, I would not thrill at spring's rebirth. The realisation had transformed the way I saw those dark and seemingly lifeless days.

Alan and I reached his Karesansui gravel garden with its jagged rocks. In these 'dry' Japanese gardens, the raked gravel represents the ripples of water, the boulders rising out of the otherwise empty space like rocky islands.

'It could be the sea with islands of rock thrusting out of the water or mountain tops emerging out of the mists,' Alan said. 'The minimalist landscapes are recreated to capture the essence of nature. They're a visual aid for meditation.'

As I was leaving, Alan gifted me a season ticket for the garden. Now, here in Derbyshire, I had access to Cascades through the seasons, the Kanrokuen Gardens I'd loved in miniature. Alan's meditation gardens shared the same Japanese design elements of Kanazawa: the intimate enclosed spaces, the asymmetrical meandering pathways and garden spaces, the symbolic planting and garden features, the harmony and balance of Japanese garden design and borrowed scenery from the surrounding cliffs and woodlands. I was grateful for Alan's gift. I promised myself I would visit the gardens through spring, summer and autumn. I would carry the gardens' themes of harmony and balance with me into the wider Peak District in the depths of our rainy winters and welcome the life-giving element of water. *The mind is everything. What you think, you become*, Buddha had said. I wasn't a Buddhist, but I understood the profound wisdom of these words. This was now my practice.

Scotland – Into the Dark, Into the Light

Nowhere is the drama of dark and light played out
more starkly than in the north.
– George Mackay Brown

Tom and I were thinking of moving north to a place where winter days are at their shortest in Britain. *Was I mad?* I wondered. I had loved the polar night of the Finnish Arctic Circle, but Scotland didn't have long-lasting snows reflecting light. Nonetheless, we'd agreed it was time to move on. Tom felt the pull of his birthplace, and I to the home of my ancestors as an Ulster Scot. We explored what we both wanted in our new home: I wanted sea close by; I wanted mountains at least marbled in snow in winter. I wanted '*the drama of dark and light played out*', as the Scottish poet George Mackay Brown wrote. Most of all, I wanted wide-open spaces that blew open the heart and mind. I wanted a landscape revealing the interplay of light and dark across vast distances. We decided we would take the campervan to spend a February week on the Fife coast and in the Cairngorms. If we could survive the cold dark days of winter in Scotland, could we not live out our days there?

When we reached the coast of Fife, winds had shaken the sea alive. Waves smashed off rocks. White horses galloped to shore. The day was bright, casting a path of light across the North Sea to Inchkeith Island. The clarity of the air was blinding, the whitewashed walls of fishing cottages too in the glassy light. The energy of the sea made my heart beat harder and faster: the swell of the tide, the suck of pebbles as the sea withdrew, the violent thrashing of water on the shore; lungfuls of spindrift. The dazzle light of the north filled my entire being with joy. There was space and an expanse of burning blue where the northern sea met the northern sky.

What was it about the ocean that drew me to it like the moon draws the tides? Was it the sense of eternality? The unending ebb and flow of water. Was it the largeness of it? The stretch of the ocean from one continent to another, great bodies of water – 70 per cent of the Earth's surface – reminding me of my place in the universe, a minuscule part in the greater scheme of the planet, but a part of it, nonetheless. Was it because the ocean, like the hills, reminded me I belonged to something much greater than me? Was it the energy of the ocean that shook me out of my stupor? Or, paradoxically, was it the singular blue of sea and sky that quietened my mind? Was it because the competing stimulation of town and city, all shouting for my attention, was reduced and simplified to a block of blue with a single song of tide? Or was it the light reflected on the surface of the sea that makes my heart sing? Absorbing the light of the ocean in the day was healing, but walking the shoreline at night, when the moon casts a silvered path across the navy, is thrilling. I thought back to one winter when Tom and I had spent a night in a treehouse set into the dunes of Tyninghame Beach in East Lothian. Back then, we'd walked the edge of the shore on the edge of winter, the sound of surf magnified in the darkness, its daytime whisper now a roar. Above our heads, the harvest moon slipped through clouds, and everything was midnight blue and white in the moonlight: the sand, the glaze of water on the shore, the sea, the sky, the clouds and surf. That night, we'd slept the sleep of the dead, shored up on the beach, encased in wood, no sound but the sea and the call of a nearby owl. I wanted more of it.

Back in the present, we inched our way along the coast, lingering in fishing villages where rusty bikes leaned against gables and anchors, painted stones and model ships adorned windows of whitewashed terraced cottages. Kinghorn, Lower Largo and Elie.

Unable to keep away from the sea, we returned to the Fife coast on the way home. At Cambo, snowdrops flooded a wooded ravine dropping to the sea. I thought of my friend Emma, who said winter finished with the first buds of snowdrops. Later, she adopted an even more extreme version, claiming winter didn't exist at all: *There are always signs of life! Really, we go straight from autumn to spring.* We'd laughed at her claims, but she had a point. Many seeds rely on winter when moisture freezes inside their cases, causing them to expand and break, then germinate in spring with the melt. Cold kills off weeds, disease, fungus, harmful bacteria and insects, playing a role in keeping plants healthy. When frosted ground melts, it irrigates soil, providing an improved air-filled structure for growing plants. Meanwhile, plants in rest mode preserve their energy, ready to burst into action in spring. I no longer saw winter's nature as dead, just in recovery mode. Did we not need to do the same as humans: rest, take stock, revitalise for spring and summer? Nature was showing me the way, helping me rewrite the narrative of winter.

In the early falling light of Fife, Tom and I *cooried* up under the duvet of the camper, listening to music, watching downloaded films, reading books, feeling cocoon-like in the tiny space of our van, sleeping through the long hours of darkness. The blackness enveloped us, comforting, not threatening. Outside, the wind gently rocked the van, the metal roof protecting us from the pinecones that came down with a soft thud. Apart from the small campsite, we were completely alone. It felt like we were the last people on Earth. It felt like the Earth belonged only to us. There was no human sound, just the quiet rustle of leaves and the low moan of wind. We were inland in this place, but it felt like we were on the high seas. In this empty corner of the country, we were beginning to realise Scotland felt right for our future.

'Shall we move here then?' I asked Tom.

'I think we should.'

By the time we returned to the coast after driving through the Cairngorms, the wind had dropped and the sea was a millpond. The light was intense on the shore, the harbours of West Wemyss and Dysart a sheet of blue, and at the same time everything was sugared in offshore mists: the east coast haar.

While the North Sea had bookended our trip, the Cairngorms were our goal. I wanted to know what its wilderness was like in the depths of winter. I had hoped to find snow, if not in the valleys at least on the heights, but this was not the case. Only the highest peaks had patches, remnants of the last fall the previous December. Temperatures were well above freezing, even on the summits. The ClimateXChange report of 2019 is depressing. There has been a marked decrease in the amount of snow lying on the Cairngorms since record-keeping began. The future is not snow-bright. And although snow cover varies from year to year, there's a general downward trend.

At Cairn Gorm, we took the Mountain Railway to reach the remains of the snowfields. Rivers of manmade snow gave skiers passage. Above the restaurant, remnants of slushy snow clung to the northern slopes. Tom and I drank coffee in the restaurant, then dropped down to the exhibition hall where a dizzying 270-degree screen laid out the Cairngorms at our feet. I saw the mountains as I'd dreamed them with a deep covering of crunch-hard snow, mile upon mile of virgin white.

But there was no virgin white as Tom and I climbed through weeks-old snow patches on the mountain and on into misted rubbles of stone on the flatted top. This was the best we could find. But from the viewing platform back at the restaurant, I realised, the snowless land had gifted me something equally alluring: a dance of dark and light. Between the dark peaty moorland, pools of brightness fell on hills and valleys. Below me, a long train of dark cloud, low in the sky, poured light from its base onto the land. Beyond, the sparkle of sea was a distant strip on the horizon. Once more, I fell in love with the clarity of the northern light. Once again, I fell in love with the expanse of space. I could breathe here. In this country – somewhere between mountain and sea – where long dark winters gives way to long, long summer days. I wanted to inhabit the darkest of rainswept days, where the light is constantly at play. Yes, without darkness, we cannot appreciate light. Without shortened days, we cannot appreciate long summer evenings. I would live out those extremes in Scotland in the *drama of dark and light*. I would continue to learn to love the dark.

Acknowledgements

Many thanks to friends in Derbyshire, who helped me through the winters: Gillian Shimwell, Emma and Ian Campbell, Brigid and Liam Frazer and Sue Corner. Particular thanks go to Olga Yezhova and her family, all of them an inspiration. Thanks go to Alan Clements too, for showing me his Japanese Zen garden in deepest Derbyshire and sharing his story with me.

Massive thanks go to the members of my writing group: Moira Ashley, Elizabeth Gowing, Joanna Griffin, Alan Packer and Katie Parry. I am indebted to Paola Fornari Hanna who proofread the entire book.

I am grateful to Visit Finland, their colleagues in Lapland and PC Agency for giving me the opportunity to visit the Arctic Circle on two occasions. Thank you to Heidi Ahvenainen for giving me a Finnish perspective on SAD. Gratitude also goes to Black Diamond and the tourist board in Japan, JNTO, making it possible for me to visit Japan – a dream come true. Thanks to JNTO's colleagues in Gifu and Ishikawa prefectures, who helped me understand *wa* – balance and harmony in all things, including the four seasons. Japan has played an important part in helping me see winter differently.

Appreciation to Michelle and Phil Munn for their continued friendship and for showing me what winter is like in Orgiva, Spain. Love to my sisters, Caroline Poole, Maggie Brooks and Audrey Wray for being there for me on my winter journeys. Unending gratitude to my husband, Tom

Moat, for being with me every step of the way – and to my sons, Jamie and Patrick Moat.

Last of all, many thanks to Sara Hunt at Saraband for her continued support and to Saraband's editor, Heather Merrick, and proofreader, Emma Rushfirth, for their diligent work.

Helen Moat is the author of *A Time of Birds* (Saraband, 2020), a travelogue of her journey across Europe by bike, with her teenage son. She has written multiple travel guides and is a regular contributor to *Derbyshire Life, BBC Countryfile* magazine, *Wanderlust*, a variety of websites and to regional radio, as well as leading travel workshops. She also contributes to several national newspapers and magazines. Originally from Northern Ireland, she lived in Derbyshire, in the heart of the Peak District National Park, for twenty-five years, before moving to Angus, Scotland, where she now lives with her husband.